South West England
Edited by Mark Richardson

First published in Great Britain in 2007 by:
Young Writers
Remus House
Coltsfoot Drive
Peterborough
PE2 9JX
Telephone: 01733 890066
Website: www.youngwriters.co.uk

All Rights Reserved

© *Copyright Contributors 2007*

SB ISBN 978-1 84602 951 8

Foreword

Young Writers was established in 1991 and has been passionately devoted to the promotion of reading and writing in children and young adults ever since. The quest continues today. Young Writers remains as committed to the nurturing of poetic and literary talent as ever.

This year's Young Writers competition has proven as vibrant and dynamic as ever and we are delighted to present a showcase of the best poetry from across the UK and in some cases overseas. Each poem has been selected from a wealth of *Little Laureates* entries before ultimately being published in this, our sixteenth primary school poetry series.

Once again, we have been supremely impressed by the overall quality of the entries we have received. The imagination, energy and creativity which has gone into each young writer's entry made choosing the poems a challenging and often difficult but ultimately hugely rewarding task - the general high standard of the work submitted ensured this opportunity to bring their poetry to a larger appreciative audience.

We sincerely hope you are pleased with this final collection and that you will enjoy *Little Laureates South West England* for many years to come.

Contents

Bathwick St Mary CE Primary School, Bath
Qianyu Liu (11)	1
Alexandra Ollendorff (10)	1
Joshua Solly (11)	2
William Moss (10)	2
William Emery (11)	3
Joshua Beresford-Browne (11)	3
Elinor Cope (11)	4
George Clark (10)	5
William Bryant (10)	6
Joseph Goodhart (10)	6
Tom Lindsay (11)	7
Amy Dixon (11)	7
Leah Rustomjee (10)	8
Katherine Wildy (10)	9
George Simonds (11)	10
Finn Tempo (10)	11
Alexander Part (11)	12
Jared Exton (11)	12
Esme Holmes-Mackie (10)	13

Charlton Kings Junior School, Cheltenham
Billy Davis (8)	13
Bradley Evans (9)	14
Jessica Brill (8)	14
Judith Richards (9)	14
Zosia Swarbrick (8)	15
Poppy Trigg (9)	15
Millie Wheeler (9)	15
Charlotte Armistead (9)	16
Nina Booth (9)	16
Ashley Hughes (9)	16
Carolina Dos Santos (9)	17
Fred Watson (8)	17
Bo Midwinter-Lean (9)	17
Jack Lancaster (8)	18
Katie Preece (8)	18
Harry Surman (9)	18

Horsington CE Primary School, Templecombe
Megan Terry (7)	19
Francesca Wagstaff (7)	19
Daisy Liddle (8)	20
Rebecca Croxton (7)	20
Harry Carnell (8)	21
George Rendell (8)	21
Harry Woolway (9)	22
Thomas Crabb (9)	22
Lauren Armson (9)	23
Toby Crabb (7)	23
Sophie Maunsell (7)	24
Alice Jackson (8)	24
Matthew Suri (7)	25
Elizabeth Ashdown (8)	25
Bradley Chant (8)	26
Anna Mylan (8)	26
Julia Wons (8)	27
Phoebe Smith (8)	27
Hugh Johnson (9)	28
Matthew Salthouse (8)	29
Ellie Martin (8)	30
Cameron Rougvie (9)	30

Newport Community School, Barnstaple
Olivia Mayne (7)	31
Alisha Leaman (7)	31
Bethany Westcott (11)	32
Alice Bennett (8)	32
Dean Bennett (8)	33
Henry Webber (8)	33
Olivia Lang (7)	34
Tom Hutchens (7)	34
Daniel Phipps (10)	35
Jess Loder (11)	35
Alice Leaman (10)	36
Billy Pennyfield (7)	36
Victoria Rushton (7)	36
Ryan Spencer (11)	37
Ellie Bayet (8)	37
Luke Draper (9)	37

Name	Score
Nathan Roode (8)	38
Philippa Bale (8)	38
Emily Cray (9)	39
Aalayah Bull (9)	39
Eleanor Smith (8)	40
Madeleine Essery (8)	40
William Flynn (8)	41
Amy Fanning (9)	41
Jessica Postles (8)	42
Jay Leaman (9)	42
Lewis Stevens (9)	43
Emily Lobb (8)	43
Molly Westcott (8)	44
Ruby Cumiskey (10)	44
Callum Platt (9)	44
Lauren White (8)	45
Emily Cawsey (11)	45
Connor Pope (8)	45
Harry Randall (9)	46
Kirsty Bennett (10)	46
Chelsea Hassan (10)	47
Ben Sherborne (10)	47
Robert Isaac (9)	48
Victoria Wood (8)	48
Brogan White (9)	49
Arianne Moore (7)	49
Zoe Stevens (9)	50
Thomas Karslake (10)	50
Emily Price (10)	50
Lucy Gill (8)	51
Hannah Underwood (10)	51
Rhiah Doldersum (8)	51
Hannah Bound (9)	52
Beth Unstead (10)	52
Chloe Macree (8)	53
Hollie Wright (10)	53
Timothy Chamings (10)	54
Rupert Beer (9)	54
Sydney Miles (9)	55
Emma Brice (10)	55
Aaron Barnes (11)	56
Aimie Footman (10)	56

Blake Ladley (10)	56
Myah Field (11)	57
Katie Ladley (11)	57
Hannah Sutton (11)	57
Alice Field (10)	58
China-Blue Pascoe (10)	58
Liam Howells (8)	59
Charlotte Rushton (11)	59
Gemma Wells (11)	60
Bradley Bell (10)	60
Nicholas Raymond (7)	60
Bradley Medhurst (10)	61
Jacob Harris (11)	61
Luke Pincombe (7)	61
Lauren Smale (7)	62
Laura Phipps (8)	62
Emily Bale (7)	62
Shane Blackmore (7)	63
Katie Harris (8)	63
Katie Shutt (8)	63
Mila Maxwell (8)	64
Martha Cumiskey (8)	64
Niamh Marshall (8)	65
Hayley McDine (7)	65
Max Kilham (8)	66
Jessica Foster (8)	66
Bethany Clarke (9)	67
Jodee Stevens (7)	67
Jamie Smith (10)	68
Tommy Hirst (7)	68
Serena Barrow (9)	69
Abigail Brock (9)	69
Chloe Medhurst (9)	70
Dean Bale (9)	70
Dale Leach (9)	71
Rhiannon Smith (9)	71
Chandler Tregaskes (10)	72
Tayler Horn (10)	72
Grace Sanders (8)	73
Chloe Mundell (9)	73
Phoebe Pethick (9)	74
Emer O'Driscoll-Paton (9)	74

Lee Barnes (9)	75
Jennifer Proctor (9)	75
Joseph Freeman (9)	76
Alfie Pennyfield (9)	76
Joseph Micklewright (9)	76
Jessica Lobb (10)	77
Lewis Walker (9)	78

Newton Ferrers CE Primary School, Plymouth

Erik Wilson (9) & Benjamin Harvey (7)	78
Nathan King, Harry Guy (8) & Imogen Tarran (9)	79
Anna Barnett & Molly Finch (8)	79
Emily Vyain (10)	80
Benjamin King (10)	81
Bryony Lawes (10)	82
Tanya Pearson & James Wall (9)	83
Jack Lake & Fergus Carruthers (8)	83
Sophie Hartley (8) & Juliet Hepburn (9)	84
Georgina McCartney (8) & Harry Honeywill (7)	84
Chloe Bruniges & Elodie Hind (7)	85

Rockwell Green CE Primary School, Rockwell Green

Emily Buttle (9)	85
Lauren Fyfe (8)	86
Ryan Pidgeon (9)	87
Hannah Druce (8)	87
Lucy May (10)	88
Kieran Martin (8)	88
Reanna Anderson (10)	89
Bethany Lowman (8)	89
Rebecca White (9)	90
Mitchell Sims (10)	90
Ben Ellins (8)	91
Owen Binding (10)	91
Georgia Dodden (9)	92
Abby Partridge (11)	92
Benedict Monteiro (8)	93
Matthew Barr (9)	93
Reegan Scotcher (9)	94
Ashleigh Dodden (9)	94
George Green (10)	95

Chelsea Baker (11)	95
Danny Morison & William Lane (10)	96
Sharnie Diston (10)	96
Molly Redstone (11)	97
Rebecca Whyte (10)	97
Jordan Webber (10)	98
Miriam Nadim (10)	98
Georgina Couzens (10)	99
Ben Ware (10)	99
Harriet Cornall (10)	100
Connie Buttle (10)	100
Rhiannon Sampson (10)	101
Samuel Buttle (11)	101
Jake Penson (11)	102
Abigail Carter (11)	102
Harry Mackenzie (10)	103
Shannon Isaacs (9)	103
Kiera Chard (10)	104
Megan Dobson (11)	104

Threemilestone School, Truro

Jack Trevail (11)	105
Fergus Laity (11)	106
Nivethitha Ram (10)	107

The Poems

Where Is My Snack?

There once was a cat,
Who was looking for his snack.
The cat's tum was already stuffed,
But he never seemed to have enough.

His fur exploded,
Like a furious pufferfish.
He may have been fluffy,
But he was very chubby.
He wouldn't go upstairs without being huffy.

Chittery, chattery,
Snickity, snackity,
Where is my snack?

Out the corner of his eye,
He saw his pie.
The eager tongue,
Jumped out with delight.

The blubbery fur ball's mouth waved,
It yawned and stretched.
And expanded into a gleeful smile.

Qianyu Liu (11)
Bathwick St Mary CE Primary School, Bath

Smile For The Camera

A smile is worth everything.

It is an upside-down frown,
A cheeky face with goofy teeth.

When you smile your face crinkles up like a round little ball.
A smile is an expression which realises happiness

So a smile lightens up the world with redeeming love.
If you smile it makes the whole world
Smile.

Alexandra Ollendorff (10)
Bathwick St Mary CE Primary School, Bath

A Smile

A smile will make you happy.
A smile will make you clappy.

A smile can stop you feeling down,
A smile is painted on the face of a clown.
A smile can chase the dark away,
A smile can make you feel so gay.

A smile will make you happy,
Even if you are still in a nappy.

A smile will not make you say.
Get out of my way.
A smile will never keep you down,
Then there is no need to frown.

Joshua Solly (11)
Bathwick St Mary CE Primary School, Bath

The Smile

The smile,
Money smiling at me,
The smile,
Funny things make me smile don't you see?
The smile,
Music makes me smile,
The smile
Running is smiling, but not once I have to run a mile.
The smile,
People are silly once they smile,
The smile,
What makes you smile?
The smile.

William Moss (10)
Bathwick St Mary CE Primary School, Bath

Smile

Behind the little blue eyes rests an inner smile.

We look for even the tiniest crack in
her little, happy smile.

We stand and look awhile. Her face full
of an innocent cuteness. But there
is no rival smile.

Upon the air which she has breathed
Is the very essence of happiness.

She rests on a comfy cushion in
her one little mind.
A small poncho covering her, head to foot.

The enormous smile written all over her.
As she plays with her little beanie baby,
A joyous smile lights up her little face.

From the little button nose, to
The eyes sparkling with
All kinds of blues, greens
And browns and the tiny speck of darkness.
But around it is the
Greatest gift of all, happiness.

William Emery (11)
Bathwick St Mary CE Primary School, Bath

Smiles

Smiles are always waiting to be worn,
If you're not happy your smile will be torn.
Smiles can be worn when talking,
But are not really made for walking.

Smiles are not to be hurt,
But can be used for eating dessert.
Happiness is the number to dial,
If you ever want to buy a smile.

Joshua Beresford-Browne (11)
Bathwick St Mary CE Primary School, Bath

My Little Fur Ball

I have a little fur ball,
He's delicate . . . in a way.
So when he came back with a broken back,
He didn't have a good day,
But still had a smile on his furry face.

His teeth, so sparkly and white,
Blink at me like the moon,
So when he got them dirty,
He cried and mimed fainting,
But still had a smile on his furry face.

Sometimes he's naughty,
It drives me *mad*,
But when I tried to catch him,
He ran to his dad,
His dad scolded him for being naughty,
But he still had a smile on his furry face.

When my fur ball,
Is ready to sleep for England,
He springs on my bed,
But he doesn't realise it's *mine*,
So I knocked him off instead,
But he still had a smile on his furry face.

So at the end of the day,
My mind is racing,
He is at the bend of my extinction,
But . . . he is my little fur ball!

Elinor Cope (11)
Bathwick St Mary CE Primary School, Bath

The Cat's Smile

An innocent cat, a grey cat;
A white cat, a furry cat, a cat
with a big . . . *smile*.
Even though you might think
he is weird. He isn't, he's a stray.

He is a cheesy cat, a Cheshire cat;
a white wide teeth cat, a guilty
cat, a wide eye cat, a cat with
a big . . . *smile*.

I found him on a street dying;
and as well he was crying as
soon as he saw me he smiled
a big cheesy smile.

You should know by now;
that it is his own emotion
now like it is his own land
of smile.

I love him and his smile;
it is his love for everyone.
He brings joy, he brings love.

His teeth are different than a
normal cat. But I know they
are white teeth and wide teeth.

Isn't my smile, it isn't your
smile, it isn't a baby's smile
it is the cat's smile.

George Clark (10)
Bathwick St Mary CE Primary School, Bath

Irish Rugby

Brave and strong. The best rugby team in the nation.

O'Driscoll is there to muller Samoa. O'Gara is there to scrape up
                                                                  the points.
Horgan is there to dive at the line as a smile appears through the mud.

They all have smiles brightly banging out from the jaw.
In training when Brian hits the bag, his teeth come smacking out
                                                                   from its cage.
When Horgan goes jogging, a cheesy grin comes over like you have
                                                          just scored a try. Do you?

Have I forgotten O'Connell? He is brave, a nose bleed doesn't hurt
                                                    although a head injury does.

The blood is dripping down looking on its past.
Blood blazes around his head but will he be alright?

When it's all over, a smile comes out of nowhere.
When they win the cup, champagne and those white, green and
orange gum shields got pulled out.
The white teeth roar out of their gleaming carnage.
That's when the best smiles show!

William Bryant (10)
Bathwick St Mary CE Primary School, Bath

A Smile

The world is corrupt.
People take bribes in cruelty.
A half-starved cat - the sign of evil.
Yet some people care and I did!
I took him in.
He miaowed the sign of need and wound himself around
My legs like a woolly scarf.
Then I smiled!
The smile on my face was true as it was clear and the
World stopped as I enjoyed my moment of happiness.

Joseph Goodhart (10)
Bathwick St Mary CE Primary School, Bath

Smile

Smile
People smile at all different things
Like when they're at school and the bell rings
Or when they're watching TV
Or even listening to the 'Little Britain' CD
And when they're at the disco
And their favourite song comes on.

Smile
A smile can brighten up someone's day
If you just give them a smile on your way
To school or when you're on holiday
Because a smile can easily change someone's day.

Tom Lindsay (11)
Bathwick St Mary CE Primary School, Bath

Smile

Little smile, little smile
Plump, podgy cheeks
Baby smile brightening up the world
With little, tiny teeth.

Big smile, big smile
Lighting up their life
Makes the world so peaceful
For both me and you.

Smiles, smiles,
We don't have to pay
For smiles like rays of sunshine
Changing those awful days.

Amy Dixon (11)
Bathwick St Mary CE Primary School, Bath

Oh Kitty When Will You Smile?

A cute, fluffy kitten,
As big as a rabbit,
No smile to spread across
Those timid lips
Why?

Everybody's got a worry,
Especially the kitty's owner
'When will a smile tickle my kitten's face?'
She worries.

People come from lands afar,
Just to make that kitten smile,
They try everything!
From frisky fish to rotten rats
To boisterous, bellowing birds.

'Oh nothing will make that kitten smile!'
The owner moans like a grumpy queen.
'We've tried everything,'
The crowd weeps!

Suddenly
The sky opens,
Puffy clouds and a deep blue sky are on show,
The sun giggles
While sunbeams dance.
A breath of fresh air glides through
The open sky.
Church bells ring.
A miracle has happened.

'Oh my,' the owner gasps.
'Finally,' the crowd cheers.
What has happened?

The kitten has finally smiled!
Angels of Heaven sing their hearts out.
The kitten's teeth gleam
As its cheesy Cheshire cat grin
Covers his face completely.
His ears prick up as the crowd cheers.
The world is now a much happier place.

A cute, fluffy kitten,
As big as a rabbit,
A smile as huge as the world itself
Spread across those timid lips.
Why?

Leah Rustomjee (10)
Bathwick St Mary CE Primary School, Bath

Smile

Big smiles, little smiles,
Light or dark,
Even small things,
Like dogs that bark.

Cute, cuddly smiles on a sunny day,
Or sad days when they are blown away,
Baby smiles are mini, adults are tall,
We even smile a lot when we're going to a ball.

Small smiles, large smiles,
Smiles all around,
Smile in the air,
Or on the ground.

Everyone can smile, even cats,
As well as elves in red and green hats,
Sometimes people smile when they are sad,
Also people smile when they are glad.

Huge smiles, tiny smiles,
Babies smile when they are three,
Everybody likes to smile,
Including you and me.

Katherine Wildy (10)
Bathwick St Mary CE Primary School, Bath

The Hunter's Smile

The alligator slipped into the still water like a knife through cheese,
The alligator set its sight on a static deer,
It sprang,
Its teeth crunched through the deer's knees,
The hunter's smile showed its razor teeth.

Like an army battalion the pack of lions advanced,
A heard of zebra grazed unaware,
The lions spread out,
They decided to begin the onslaught,
The hunter's smile lay down after a hefty meal.

The carnage attracted the sharks like magnets,
A dying seal swam frantically just below the surface
The shark sped southward towards the struggling seal,
The blubber felt superbly scrumptious in the shark's mouth,
The hunter's smile was covered in blood.

The harsh call of African hunters is an eagle's cry when searching for food,
The traps trickled with deer's blood,
They threw their spears at the dying deer
The speedy spear pierced the pale deer's skin,
The hunter's smile grinned with happiness.

The hunter's smile keeps predators alive!

George Simonds (11)
Bathwick St Mary CE Primary School, Bath

The Smile Of Shannara

Shea Shannara was smiling sweetly
But down in the dark, dreary vale
A battle raged, up high, fiercely
A battle for the southland, we shall not prevail

But one of Shea's smiling servants
Had heard of this huge battle.
And warned the young monarch of the conflicts.
Worry, he did not for he could smile.

But the battle moved west.
'We're losing, to Tyrsis,' we go.
Where are the dwarves to the east?
Or the Elves. Do they come? No.

Hey, look! From Tyrsis comes something worthwhile.
Some Elvin travellers are coming this way.
They are bearing a smile.
The trolls and gnomes are turning away.

My friends! You cannot win by force.
No, swords cannot win an invasion.
A sword cannot destroy a troll, gnome or Norse.
A smile is ten times better than any weapon.

Finn Tempo (10)
Bathwick St Mary CE Primary School, Bath

My Brother

His smile is like no other.
Thick and chubby like a block of cheese.
When he laughs, he laughs like a lion
Strong and powerful like a gust of wind.

As he opens his deep brown eyes
Laser beams shoot out from all areas.
His hair long and lashing in the wind.
Blond and bold, knotted and tangled like a knotted rope.

His cheeks rosy and red.
His lips powerful and crimson.
And as he smiles so gently it feels like a
Breeze of wind.

My brother is a kind loving soul,
Like no other.

Alexander Part (11)
Bathwick St Mary CE Primary School, Bath

Mind Of Peace

There's a place within myself
where the grass is green, the sky is pink
and glass stairs lead to floating beds.
There, a smile is the only expression.

It's a land where war and hatred
are just words.
And a smile is spread across
everyone's face.

It's a place where I go when the real world's too much
It's nice because its feeling makes me smile.

It's a place of joy, it's a place of happiness, it's a place of laughter
and it is called my mind.

Jared Exton (11)
Bathwick St Mary CE Primary School, Bath

Baby Smile

Bubbly smiles,
Wide smiles,
One-tooth smiles,
Chubby cheeks!

Silly smiles,
Sweet smiles,
Cute smiles,
Chubby cheeks!

Ugly smiles,
Shy smiles,
Scrunched-up smiles,
Chubby cheeks!

Sunny smiles,
Cheesy smiles,
Wonky smiles,
Chubby cheeks!

Esme Holmes-Mackie (10)
Bathwick St Mary CE Primary School, Bath

China

C elebrating Chinese New Year is amazing.
H ighest mountains settle there.
I ts capital is the wonderful Beijing.
N ot very many giant pandas, they're very, very rare.
A nd in Beijing they have a huge central square, which is the biggest in the world and is called Tiananmen Square.

Billy Davis (8)
Charlton Kings Junior School, Cheltenham

China

C hina's coastline is over 18,000km long.
H ong Kong is very close to China.
I n the centre of Beijing is the largest public square.
N i hao means hello in Chinese Mandarin.
A wooden frame called an abacus is used to work out sums.

Bradley Evans (9)
Charlton Kings Junior School, Cheltenham

China

C hinese people are very fond of tea.
H ong King is very close to China.
I n China most people speak Mandarin.
N i hao means hello in China.
A bout 30 million bikes are produced each year in China.

Jessica Brill (8)
Charlton Kings Junior School, Cheltenham

China

C hina is a beautiful country to visit.
H imalayas has a rare animal called a yak within.
I n China, kite flying is very popular.
N i hao means hello in Chinese Mandarin.
A bout 30 million bikes are produced every year.

Judith Richards (9)
Charlton Kings Junior School, Cheltenham

China

C hina is estimated to be about the size of Europe!
H ong Kong is very near to China!
I n China they celebrate a day called Chinese New Year!
N ow China has more places to visit and more sights to see!
A wooden frame called an abacus is still used today in China!

Zosia Swarbrick (8)
Charlton Kings Junior School, Cheltenham

China

C hina produces 30 million bikes each year.
H undreds of people in China sleep at lunchtime
I n the centre of Beijing is Tiananmen Square
N i hao means hello in Mandarin.
A Chinese person has to learn 50 thousand picture symbols, which make the Chinese language.

Poppy Trigg (9)
Charlton Kings Junior School, Cheltenham

China

C hina is about the size of Europe put together.
H imalayas is a mountain and on its land lives the ox.
I n Chinese schools after lunch young pupils go to sleep.
N ow giant pandas are very rare and live in Suchan Forest.
A cupuncture is a traditional Chinese medical treatment.

Millie Wheeler (9)
Charlton Kings Junior School, Cheltenham

China

C hina is a very big country.
H ong Kong is really close to China.
I n China they have tall buildings.
N ow China has old and new buildings.
A Chinese penny is valuable.

Charlotte Armistead (9)
Charlton Kings Junior School, Cheltenham

China

C hina's capital is Beijing,
H aving a kite is a popular thing,
I n China they make lots of cool toys,
N ow don't get sad, they're for both girls and boys.
A nd on New Year's Day always say 'Gung hey fat choi!'

Nina Booth (9)
Charlton Kings Junior School, Cheltenham

China

C hina is as big as all of Europe.
H ello in Chinese is ni hao.
I n China you speak Cantonese or Mandarin.
N ow you'll see there's hardly any litter I bet.
A nd the amount of bicycles you'll never forget!

Ashley Hughes (9)
Charlton Kings Junior School, Cheltenham

China

C hina is developing as we move.
H ong Kong is on the edge of China.
I n China there are pandas.
N orth of Xian, the Terracotta Army is found.
A cupuncture is a traditional Chinese treatment.

Carolina Dos Santos (9)
Charlton Kings Junior School, Cheltenham

China

C hina's largest lake is the super-big Qinghai.
H ave a look at the Terracotta, defending the tomb of Qin-Shi-Huangdi.
I n China you will find your dream holiday.
N i hao is how to say hello to everybody every day!
A cupuncture is a Chinese medical treatment with many needles.

Fred Watson (8)
Charlton Kings Junior School, Cheltenham

China

C hina make three fifths of the world's shoes.
H ong Kong is very close to China.
I n China most people speak Mandarin.
N i hao means hello in Mandarin.
A bsolutely everyone in China has a job!

Bo Midwinter-Lean (9)
Charlton Kings Junior School, Cheltenham

China

C hina is about the size of Europe.
H ong Kong is attached to China.
I n China their favourite sport is table tennis.
N i hao means hello in Chinese Mandarin.
A cupuncture is a traditional Chinese treatment.

Jack Lancaster (8)
Charlton Kings Junior School, Cheltenham

China

C hina is quite busy and is pretty.
H ello in Mandarin is ni hao.
I n China they have the Great Wall and is 6,700km long.
N o one has seen such a wonderful place.
A t some Chinese schools they have different clothing for every day.

Katie Preece (8)
Charlton Kings Junior School, Cheltenham

China

C hina's coastline is over 18,000km long.
H ong Kong is very close to China and they can speak Mandarin.
I n China 'ni hao' means hello.
N orth of Xian, the Terracotta Army is found.
A bout 30 million bikes are made each year.

Harry Surman (9)
Charlton Kings Junior School, Cheltenham

The Creaking Door

A creaking door slowly opens,
A slow walk is heard,
A black box splits open on the dining table,
A black cat keyring is found inside,
A tiny hand grabs the shiny keys,
A squeaky voice screams,
A large dog growls,
A tiny shell sticks to the walking shoe,
A car screeches to a stop outside,
A bright key slips onto the tray,
A ghostly hand picks up the key,
A ripping sound comes from the wooden crate,
Turning the key in the crate's lock,
The creaking lid slowly opens,
Inside there are two bodies!

Megan Terry (7)
Horsington CE Primary School, Templecombe

The Dark Cave

Whenever you go for a lonely walk,
Watch and listen to the dark noises,
Wailing ghosts and hooting owls,
Crunching gravel and moaning stairs.

Banging windows and creaking doors,
Sweeping bats and dripping caves
On your lonely walk.
Take care!

Francesca Wagstaff (7)
Horsington CE Primary School, Templecombe

Haunted House

On top of Scary Hill there's an isolated haunted house.
It gives me nightmares when I sleep.
The ghost there is as white as a sheet
His name is Hector -
Hector the spectre.
As for the house he lives in,
It's a terrible state it's like
Spectacular Dracula has just had a party!
Cobwebs hang from shattered windows,
Broken glass litters the old floor.
Surprisingly, Hector loves it there!
Just guess what his favourite food is . . .
Heinz blood surprise!
So stay away from Hector
Stay away from his friends.
Spooky, Sokie and Big Mak,
Stay away from danger.

Daisy Liddle (8)
Horsington CE Primary School, Templecombe

The Ghost House

My scary ghost enjoys haunting
My fluffy cat and ancient house
He moves the food and furniture,
But most of all he likes to sleep
On my bouncy bed.
He's really kind and gentle,
He loves to play in the beautiful garden
He can be lots of fun
But when he sees his spooky friends
He tries to scare me silly!

Rebecca Croxton (7)
Horsington CE Primary School, Templecombe

The Ghost Underground

Deep underground
Locked in a damp prison cell
Was a creepy ghost.
It smashed and bashed the metal bars.
The evil ghost was becoming angry.
The scary ghost was making his plans
And was going to escape his cell.
He waited for it to become dark.
A group of girls knocked the oak door
And the butler answered.
The angry ghost waited until everyone fell asleep.
Once the dark house was all quiet
The underground ghost knocked the door down.
He made his way upstairs,
There was a crash
The scared girls screamed, 'Argh!'
Next there was a thud,
'He's dead!'

Harry Carnell (8)
Horsington CE Primary School, Templecombe

Creepy House

Ancient and ruined,
The haunted house stands
In the winds of Hell.
In the howling wind
Rushes through the empty house.
The terrified man is caught
By the fierce wind.
He walks the corridors
Alone at midnight.

George Rendell (8)
Horsington CE Primary School, Templecombe

Slippery Shadow House

One dark afternoon
a little boy walked
to the derelict house,
Slippery Shadow Manor
had been a ruin for many years.
Slowly the young boy
walked up the long driveway,
each step made
a crunching sound on the gravel,
At the entrance
he pulls on the bell
and inside a chime is heard echoing.
The ghostly butler opens the door.
The ghoulish butler shows the boy in.
The ghoulish butler says, 'Enjoy your stay!'
As he walks through the ancient door,
exploring the manor
the boy sees
the ghost of Slippery Shadow Manor.
Turning white with fright
the scared boy runs from the house!

Harry Woolway (9)
Horsington CE Primary School, Templecombe

Deadly Night

It has come, the deadliest night of the spooky year,
The ancient clock smashes on the floor.

The blood sucking ghouls
Have time to scare and kill tonight,
The creaking of the wooden door
I try to ignore.

The glowing skeleton with gleaming sword and blinding red eyes,
Opens its dark cape and Mummy cries, 'You silly boy!'

Thomas Crabb (9)
Horsington CE Primary School, Templecombe

The Ghost Catcher

'Argh!' the annoying grunt is heard again,
Trying to catch the unsuspecting ghosts and end their days.
Moaning ghosts horrifying the human race
Call the ghost catcher again.

All the terrifying ghosts are wailing,
Scurrying around
When the bloodsucking monster appears.

The deadly ghost catcher is the ugliest man you could imagine.
He's mean, frightening and cruel.
His magical weapon is a silver net,
With one flick of the deadly net
The frightened ghosts are caught
Beware the deadly ghost catcher!
Shooting out of chimneys like rockets
Appearing slowly through stone walls.

Lauren Armson (9)
Horsington CE Primary School, Templecombe

Under The Bed Ghost

Under my bed, in the dark
A tiny ghost is hiding,
Is the minute ghost mean and scary?
What could it be hiding?
With my old cuddly toys and ripped books.
Dirty grey socks and a broken pencil,
It can't be fun!
Slowly the bedroom door opens.

I rush into the cold room,
The creaking door slams!
I search for my little ghost
But he's disappeared
Or so I think,
But what is that scurrying?

Toby Crabb (7)
Horsington CE Primary School, Templecombe

The Weird Ghost

In a deep dark wood
with scary bats and black
birds swooping over your head.
Wait I can hear wailing and
booing ahead.

I see something in the distance,
with a white,
ripped sheet and dark black eyes.

Then *boo!*
We know that's a spooky ghost.
Then the screaming ghost
vanished into a dark abandoned
haunted house.

Sophie Maunsell (7)
Horsington CE Primary School, Templecombe

Haunted House!

In a dark, spooky house,
a tiny ghost is there.
It is a miniature ghost with,
black beady eyes and a
deadly body!

It likes to creep,
around all night long.
But when the friendly people come along,
it likes to hide.

It is a dark massive house,
I wonder how it can see?
The brown huge house,
as tall as it can be!

Alice Jackson (8)
Horsington CE Primary School, Templecombe

Phantom Menace

In a gloomy street called Haunted Road,
there is a shack with a creaking door with rusty hinges.

Inside the shack there is a phantom
with menacing red eyes and sharp pointed teeth
and blood trickling down his gleaming white sheet.

Bloodthirsty monster,
deadly frightening,
yelling and screaming.

Then all goes quiet
he hears some children creeping to the door,
here was his chance!

Quietly he drifts through the window
and floats behind the children!

'Ahh!' screams James
John turns around,
he sees James' helpless legs dangling around,
around like twigs on a tree,
with bony and bloody tears on his jeans.

Then he sees . . .
the Phantom Menace.

Matthew Suri (7)
Horsington CE Primary School, Templecombe

The Ghost Hunt

Creak goes the door as some howling ghosts come in.
Then suddenly I am surrounded by scary ghosts.
They howl like wolves and breathe like ice.
Rattle goes the window as another ghost arrives.
It looks like the leader of
The ghost hunt!

Elizabeth Ashdown (8)
Horsington CE Primary School, Templecombe

Haunted House

The old haunted house
Stood flapping in the wind.
The old creepy staircase
Chunks of steps and rails missing.

The deadly vampires
Hiding in the cupboard.
The wailing of the ghost
Would really make you shiver!

The clanking of the chain ghost
Would make you stop still.
Blood dripping from the roof
Making a red puddle on the floor!

The creaking of the wooden floor panels
And the old wooden door
Banging on its hinges in the wind!

Bradley Chant (8)
Horsington CE Primary School, Templecombe

The Church Ghost!

Beyond Charlton Hawthorne there is a deadly haunted church.
It's so awfully old there are no pretty flowers just dead trees!
There are hundreds of scratched graves
Where patient people do their prayers.
Now it is midnight
The see-through church ghost appears.
But the church ghost doesn't spook alone,
With him he has three friends,
One small, one tall and one really greedy ghost!
Keep out of the horrid church
Or you *will . . . die!*

Anna Mylan (8)
Horsington CE Primary School, Templecombe

Ghost Time

In an ancient, crumbling house,
lived a sweet, small mouse.

It was finishing a mouldy apple core,
when a wailing ghost came in at the door.

It shrieked out in terror,
when the naughty ghost made an error
and followed the poor mouse up the wall.

When the young mouse warned everyone,
that the freaky ghost wasn't gone,
they got out the mint soap from the first time.

The end of the transparent ghost,
came very quickly and close,
when the terrified people squirted him
with their deadly soap.

Julia Wons (8)
Horsington CE Primary School, Templecombe

Ghost

In the deadly cemetery there are some scary gravestones.
Past the spooky tombstones there is a terrifying house.
In the waiting manor house there is a dark, dark staircase.
Down the dark shattered staircase there is an antique door,
Open the door and you will find a . . . frightening *ghost!*
The terrifying ghost is very spooky,
Its ghostly sheet made me jump.
It is so transparent all that can be seen is its . . . *chains!*

Phoebe Smith (8)
Horsington CE Primary School, Templecombe

Grave Dweller

The silent hillside held many secrets,
Unpleasant but true.
The isolated marshland, the imprisoned hill,
The smell of old flesh, William's kill.

Hastings stood silent, old and still,
Dying of its memories, saddened by its kill.

Then it happened, a deafening roar,
And then to their horror, the whole of England saw.

In their dreams Harold stood his ground,
Like a weary bloodshot hound.

His red eyes burnt with anger, burnt with hate,
Astonished by William, astonished by his fate.

Suddenly the soaking marshland rumbled,
Arrows stuck up, their cloaks were drowned,
Their silent faces were blank.

Their axes hung loose, their transparent shields were mouldy dirt.
Dead men woke up, wanted revenge.

They ruined the nearby delicate villages with their
                             blood-covered swords,
Burgled the jewels, killed the mighty lords.

So watch out for the great terrors of the past,
That thought may be your very last!

Hugh Johnson (9)
Horsington CE Primary School, Templecombe

The Ghostly Howl

One spooky night at midnight,
I heard a ghostly howl,
it sounded like a real scary howl.

So I crept out of my best bed
and ran down the stairs.

I put my Scooby-Doo slippers on
and skipped out and guess what I saw?
A scary *phantom!*

The phantom looked as if he had come
from mighty Mars.

It had two eyes like boulders and two mouths,
no nose and five ears
most scary and last of all
it had two heads!

Or maybe he had come from the
mountains of Scotland.

I could not describe him completely
I am not telling you why but I ran upstairs
and hid under the duvet.

And then I heard a low moaning
growl echoing through the night . . .

Matthew Salthouse (8)
Horsington CE Primary School, Templecombe

The Haunted Trees

Slowly walking to an old school
the frightened children
notice the dark trees.
Listening, the children hear
the hooting of owls,
rustling leaves and swooping bats,
squirrels scurrying through the trees
to collect chestnuts
that have fallen onto the damp ground.
Suddenly a wailing sound
comes from the dark trees.
Unexpectedly a pair of red eyes are seen,
a scary ghost jumps out of the dark trees
scaring them away.

Ellie Martin (8)
Horsington CE Primary School, Templecombe

Ghost

All the lonely ghost wanted was close friends,
He floated over to the playing children,
But they just ran away.
He vanished and reappeared
In his cold, damp castle,
And he laid down on his spiky bed and cried.
He heard a clanking sound
Which made him jump with fear,
He slowly crept towards the wailing sound,
And wished the noise would disappear.
A young intruder tripped on the stone stairs
And the noise echoed around,
Once the adventurous boy
Saw the castle's ghost appear and wail
He soon disappeared!

Cameron Rougvie (9)
Horsington CE Primary School, Templecombe

Giggle Higgle

Silly songs make me laugh,
Shout and jump and wriggle;
But most of all they make me giggle.
Clapping hands,
Waving them around,
Jump up high and then
Do the splits on the ground.
Wiggling hips,
Fast, then slow,
This way, that way
Watch me go;
Happy and jolly,
Stamping feet,
Hit the floor
In time with the beat;
Silly songs make me
Want to jiggle,
But all I really want to do
Is giggle and giggle.

Olivia Mayne (7)
Newport Community School, Barnstaple

My Dreams

My dreams are to be on stage
Singing my heart out,
Being a second Julie Andrews.
If not, I would love to work in a hotel
Serving the dinners, especially at Christmas.
But if it's not any of them
I will just be happy with what I get.

Alisha Leaman (7)
Newport Community School, Barnstaple

Sweet Dreams

S nuggled up in your cosy bed
W aiting until it's dark to see the stars;
E nergy is wearing off now you're asleep;
E xciting dreams exploring your mind;
T urn off the bedtime lamp.

D ancing dreams running around,
R eady to dream in a wonder world;
E nter a land of mythical . . .
A mazing creatures yet to be discovered.
M agical things happen when you're in bed;
S till dreaming, please don't wake me yet!

Bethany Westcott (11)
Newport Community School, Barnstaple

Dance

Dance is fun, dance is wild,
Lots of fun for
Me and you.

Sometimes dance is
Slow and graceful
Like ballet.

I only like the fast dances
Like jazz and
Modern.

Now you know dance
Is great, come along
And have some fun!

Alice Bennett (8)
Newport Community School, Barnstaple

The Wind

Trees swaying,
Dustbins clattering,
Destroyed branches,
Twigs snapping,
Roofs flying,
Flowers bending,
Green seas,
Grass flowing,
Footballs rolling,
Stones moving,
Houses falling,
Signs breaking.

Dean Bennett (8)
Newport Community School, Barnstaple

Big Cats

At night tigers are hunting
When they've finished they start panting.

Lions have very long fangs,
When they've hunted they come home in gangs.

Jaguars lie in trees,
If they rub other animals they get fleas.

Snow leopards live in the snow,
Sometimes they go very slow.

Black panthers run very fast
When they're at top speed they go zooming past!

Henry Webber (8)
Newport Community School, Barnstaple

When I Go To The Zoo

I love a trip to the zoo,
Why don't you come along too?

The hippos playing in the mud,
While elephants walk by with a thud.

The lion gives out a mighty roar,
In the next cage was the wild boar.

The flamingos have a soft, calm dance,
And the horse in the paddock gives a big prance.

We go inside to see the snake,
Then we have a boat ride on the flowing lake.

The giraffes stretch up with their very long neck,
While the ducks swim by with a peck, peck, peck.

The monkeys are all being very cheeky,
And the reptiles are very sneaky.

Time to go home and have some tea.
Thank you for coming to the zoo with me.

Olivia Lang (7)
Newport Community School, Barnstaple

My Brother's New Bike

My brother has got a bike,
He got it for his birthday,
It's brand new from the shop,
He jumps on it, and he's away.

He rides on it to Braunton,
He does wheelies and big jumps,
It's the best he's ever had
He whizzes over bumps.

Tom Hutchens (7)
Newport Community School, Barnstaple

Football Crazy

F ast, furious
O ut the way!
O uch! That hurt.
T urn and run.
B ack to me,
A t last a chance,
L ost the ball!
L ongest pass ever!

C ollect the ball,
R un, pass,
A cross. Attack we're on our way.
Z ola! It's his,
Y es, yes, yes, *it's a goal!*

Daniel Phipps (10)
Newport Community School, Barnstaple

Bullies

Bullies, bullies, bullies,
Who do they think they are?
Bullies, bullies, bullies,
From here and afar.

Bullies, bullies, bullies,
Not nice to meet,
Bullies, bullies, bullies,
Together we defeat.

Bullies, bullies, bullies,
We know what they are,
Bullies, bullies, bullies,
Cowards are what they are.

Jess Loder (11)
Newport Community School, Barnstaple

My Niece And Nephews

My niece and nephews are -
little tinkers
very funny
great cuddlers
because they're chubby.
One shouts *Dadda* at everything
one's a Bob the Builder lover
and his sister, a big bum nic nic shower!
but everything about them I love them to bits.
Nearly my next niece due
my poor brother with all that poo!

Alice Leaman (10)
Newport Community School, Barnstaple

When I Go Out To Play

When I go out to play
Children shouting, wind blowing;
When I go out to play,
Bushes moving, gates slamming;
When I go out to play
Doors banging, balls rolling.

Billy Pennyfield (7)
Newport Community School, Barnstaple

Summer

S hining sun up in the sky
U mbrellas to shade you instead of the rain
M ake a drink to cool you down
M ust go to the beach to have some fun
E veryone loves to swim in the sea
R elaxing because school's over.

Victoria Rushton (7)
Newport Community School, Barnstaple

My Dog Storm

Tail wagging,
Mad barking,
Hand licking,
Bone chewing,
Cat chasing,
Firework hating,
Fast running,
Fun loving.

Ryan Spencer (11)
Newport Community School, Barnstaple

School

School is lots of fun,
School is sometimes great,

School is usually boring,
School is sometimes very hard,

School is always cheerful,
With lots of friends to play with!

Ellie Bayet (8)
Newport Community School, Barnstaple

The Weather

The sun is brighter than a light,
The rain is wetter than a dripping tap,
The wind is howling like a wild dog;
The kind of day to be in the warm,
All huddled by the fire.

Luke Draper (9)
Newport Community School, Barnstaple

My Brother Tom

My brother Tom bites his nails;
My brother Tom stamps on snails;
My brother Tom gets lots of merits;
My brother Tom loves his ferrets;
My brother Tom loves Man U.
My brother Tom spends ages in the loo;
My brother Tom really loves me;
My brother Tom is so funny;
My brother Tom is not so bad;
He's my brother Tom, and for that I'm glad.

Nathan Roode (8)
Newport Community School, Barnstaple

Fire, Fire

Stacked high,
flames light,
coal dark,
flames dance,
fire, fire.

Wood hot.
flames run,
fire crackles,
flames yellow,
fire, fire.

Smoke dark,
flames flash,
ash falls,
flames die
no more fire.

Philippa Bale (8)
Newport Community School, Barnstaple

I'm The Angel

I have two annoying sisters;
Their names are Darcie and Libby.
They are younger than me
And are *so* silly.
Whenever Libby has tomatoes she squashes them;
But I'm the angel!

We squabble and we fight,
But I'm always right.
When we play there's always a mess
And my mum gets really stressed;
It's *never* me who makes it untidy
But it's always me who makes it tidy;
And it's just not fair
Because I'm the angel!

Mum and Dad love us all
But are glad (sometimes)
When we are at school.
The house is quiet,
No squabbling at all.
But I'm still the angel!

Emily Cray (9)
Newport Community School, Barnstaple

Flowers

F oxgloves found in a field;
L ovely lilac lilies lounge lazily;
O range blossom overgrowing in an orchard;
W eeping willows whisper wildly;
E lephants eat elderflowers every day;
R ed roses ramble round rocky ruins;
S weet peas sing a sweet song.

Aalayah Bull (9)
Newport Community School, Barnstaple

My Dog

Phoebe's wet nose tells me.
She's as happy as can be.

My puppy plays in the afternoon sun.
Chasing the ball she's full of fun.

Her curly soft ears are long and black.
She likes to beg for a tasty snack.

Her loving brown eyes, sparkle in the light.
They make her look so very bright.

My muddy dog needs a bath.
She tires to splash out, it makes me laugh.

After a bath she's not so smelly.
She can sit on my lap and watch the telly.

She's sometimes naughty but I don't mind.
I love my puppy because she is kind.

Eleanor Smith (8)
Newport Community School, Barnstaple

Chocolate

C hocolate is great, creamy and delicious;
H ave fun with melting chocolate;
O range inside, strawberry inside, crunchy inside,
C hocolate is gorgeous with all sorts of insides;
O ver the years chocolate has become famous;
L ovely chocolate. Yum! Yum!
A treat for everyone.
T ea is chocolate every night (I wish!)
E at chocolate now!

Madeleine Essery (8)
Newport Community School, Barnstaple

My Brother

Luke's favourite for dinner
Chicken, broccoli and sprouts
The sprouts are footballs
Which he kicks about.

At 7pm he causes mayhem
Flooding the floor up to the door,
His smiling face while in the bath,
Thinking about throwing a toy at his dad.

Lukie is in his pyjamas getting
Ready for bed. He drinks his milk
And cleans his teeth
And then he's off to bed.

My little cute brother Lukie Bear.

William Flynn (8)
Newport Community School, Barnstaple

The Mysterious Land Of Dreams

Silver-lined clouds in pale pink sky,
Dashed with the faintest blue;
Snowy white unicorns flying gently in the air,
Coming to visit me and you.
Fairies flying silently around,
Their footsteps making not a sound.
Pixies and goblins making mischief,
Dancing round a moonlit leaf.
A land surrounded by twinkling streams;
Now this is my land of mysterious dreams.

Amy Fanning (9)
Newport Community School, Barnstaple

The Beach

Our bags are packed
For a day at the beach.
Climbing down pebbles
The waves within reach.

Look at the surfers
Riding the crest of the waves
See the bobbing boats
Appearing through the haze.

Sun beaming down
On the golden sands,
Mummy running to me
With suncream in her hands.

Feeling rather hungry
Looking forward to lunch,
What's that flying above?
A flock of seagulls ready to munch!

The sun is now setting,
The colour - a deep red,
I'm feeling rather tired now,
I'm ready for my bed.

Jessica Postles (8)
Newport Community School, Barnstaple

My Island

My island has a cheeky little monkey
That dances around the hot, exotic beach.
A nice relaxing cocktail drink
That cools me down;
The whistle when the wind
Hits the beautiful palm trees.
These are the things
I like on my island.

Jay Leaman (9)
Newport Community School, Barnstaple

Families

Families can be big
Families can be small;
Every family is different.

Some have brothers, some have sisters,
Some have aunties, some have uncles,
Some have half-brothers or stepsisters;
Some even have foster or adopted children.
Every family is different.

Some families fall out,
Some families annoy one another,
Some families play together quite nicely
And love one another.
Every family is different.

My family has five people;
One sister, one half-brother,
A lovely mum, a crazy dad and normal me;
We all fall out, we all annoy one another,
We all play together, but most of all
We love one another.
Every family is different.

Lewis Stevens (9)
Newport Community School, Barnstaple

Our Rabbits

My sister and I have two lovely bunnies,
Mine is so cute, and her name is Honey;
She is sandy white and fluffy, with a little wet nose;
I have to be careful or she will nibble my toes.

Freckles is brown with a little white tummy,
She makes me giggle because she's awfully funny;
She hops, jumps and plays in the garden for an hour,
But Daddy gets cross when she eats all his flowers.

Emily Lobb (8)
Newport Community School, Barnstaple

Swimming

S wimming up and down lengths of the pool
W hich stroke is up to you
I n your swimsuit you look cool
M aybe a bikini
M aybe a tankini
I t doesn't matter
N ever mind that let's play
G reat fun for you, hooray!

Molly Westcott (8)
Newport Community School, Barnstaple

School Dinners

Broccoli, cabbage, carrots, asparagus,
Healthy food they stuff inside of us;
Jamie Oliver has a lot to answer for,
I didn't ask him to knock on our school's door.

Fruit and veg coming out of our ears,
All to satisfy the government's fears;
All I want is to make the turkey twizzle
And then I will stop all this hungry grizzle.

Ruby Cumiskey (10)
Newport Community School, Barnstaple

My Guinea Pig

My guinea pig is called Ellie,
She has a rather big belly,
She lives in our house,
She is a lot like a mouse
Except she is not that small.
My guinea pig is very clever
Ellie is my best friend ever.

Callum Platt (9)
Newport Community School, Barnstaple

Puppies

Puppies are cute like a ball of fluff,
Eyes that shine like a light,
Noses that glisten, paws that are mucky,
Fur that is soft like a woolly jumper;
Their tails wag with excitement,
Their bodies shiver with fear,
They run around the house and chew slippers;
They sleep curled up in their baskets.
That's what puppies are like.

Lauren White (8)
Newport Community School, Barnstaple

Dolphins

Soaring through the ocean
As graceful as a swan;
When it comes to playful fish
They are number one.
Some have bottle noses,
They swim around in a school,
They jump in and out of
A clear, blue pool.

Emily Cawsey (11)
Newport Community School, Barnstaple

Fluffy Bunnies

Run, fluffy rabbit, run;
Play around and have some fun.
Dance around all day long,
Fluffy little tails, soft and cuddly,
They sunbathe in the sun.

Connor Pope (8)
Newport Community School, Barnstaple

My Puppies

One black and white,
One white and brown,
Two bundles of fun bounding around.
Fighting and biting and playing all day;
Picking toys up that get in my way;
Two little rascals who are rather sweet,
But not very nice when they're biting my feet;
With feeding and walkies all through the day,
Mopping and sweeping their parcels away.
Their cute little faces I see each day,
I'll be their best friend all the way;
Nelly and Ben are their names,
Fun and mess is their game!

Harry Randall (9)
Newport Community School, Barnstaple

Teachers

Teachers of English
Teachers of maths
Teachers of PE
Teachers of computers

They are great
And really funny
With a smile upon
Their face

Teaching us what we need to know
Getting us to do our best
With a smile upon their face.

Kirsty Bennett (10)
Newport Community School, Barnstaple

Sugar Plum Fairy

I live in the woods so far away,
And never ever get time to play,
I have no family, I have no friends,
And everywhere I go it leads to dead-ends.

Animals are so scary,
Because I am a little sugar plum fairy,
Days are so short nights are so long
And the wind and the rain goes on.

Bluebells are blossoming,
Spring is round the corner,
I wish I could just be a little girl
Who is loved by her family.

Chelsea Hassan (10)
Newport Community School, Barnstaple

The Spot

My dad had a spot
On the side of his face,
It wasn't just a dot
It was a perfect disgrace.

So what could he do
To be rid of this thing
That was causing such a to-do,
And making his face sting?

So he found some cream
And it didn't make him scream,
And very soon it would disappear
And his face would be all clear.

Ben Sherborne (10)
Newport Community School, Barnstaple

Football Match

When the stadium is full,
and the people all cheer,
the players are jumping
and excited that kick-off is near.

When the referee's whistle blows,
the players are ready, while the children
at home are hugging their teddies.

When the line-up is picked
and the ball is kicked,
the players have gum in
their mouth and it keeps being licked.

When it's half-time,
the players eat their lime,
while in the dressing room the
players are singing a nursery rhyme.

When the match is all over,
some of the players go back to Dover,
While the manager drives back
in his Land Rover.

Robert Isaac (9)
Newport Community School, Barnstaple

Max

Max is my dog, and he is cute;
He is hairy and fluffy and huge;
Max is a German Shepherd;
White, black and tan,
He has pointy ears, big teeth and a long, wet nose.
He is very strong and silly.
He chases his tail,
He is licky and loving and sleeps a lot;
Max is my dog and he is cute.

Victoria Wood (8)
Newport Community School, Barnstaple

Friends

All my friends mean
A lot to me, there's
Serena, Hollie and
Of course Ezzie.
When we walk and
When we talk they
Make me laugh, they
Make me giggle, I'm
A small person in the middle.

On non-school uniform
Day we were playing
It and the boys were
Wearing their football kit;
When we were doing maths
All together we were trying to be clever.

I like maths and art
Both together. I will like them
For ever and ever.
This was my poem about
School and friends.
Now my poem ends.

Brogan White (9)
Newport Community School, Barnstaple

Flowers

Bright red roses,
Really green weeds.

The tiniest daffodils,
You've ever seen.

They grown in the garden,
And sometimes on trees.

Sometimes just like blossom,
And bees come and go whenever they please.

Arianne Moore (7)
Newport Community School, Barnstaple

Snow

Snow covers the land in white silk,
Snow flutters slowly to the ground,
Snow is the colour of white creamy milk,
Crunch, crunch snow makes a sound,
Snow shimmers in the sunlight,
Snow, you can throw around,
Snow gives you a frosty, bitter bite,
With snow, you can make a mound,
Snow, eventually, melts away,
But you never know,
It may come another day.

Zoe Stevens (9)
Newport Community School, Barnstaple

Pirates

P irates are always robbing
I n and out of fights
R umbling through hidden treasure
A lways ready to steal
T errorising lots of ships
E very day there is lots more treasure
S words and pistols at the ready.

Thomas Karslake (10)
Newport Community School, Barnstaple

A Toothpick

A toothpick
Is a stick
It's made of wood,
And it picks out your food;
It picks out beef
When it's stuck in your teeth.

Emily Price (10)
Newport Community School, Barnstaple

In Spring

In spring
April showers become glittering rainbows.
In spring
Newborn lambs start to become fluffy, puffy sheep.
In spring
Kites soar in the sky on a windy day.
In spring
A bulb stretches out its stem which sprouts into a red tulip.
In spring
Grey skies become light blue.

Lucy Gill (8)
Newport Community School, Barnstaple

Weather

Weather, isn't it just full of emotion?
I mean, one minute it's sunny and the next minute it's rain;
Gale force winds, now they are the UK's wrestling champions;
They are like a mad pack of dogs that are desperate for food;
Hurricanes and tornadoes are world wrestling champions;
They are ten dominant male bears, scavenging predators;
Thunderstorms are as loud as an overwrought elephant's cry;
The lightning is as eye-blinding as the winter sun.

Hannah Underwood (10)
Newport Community School, Barnstaple

Lullaby

No monsters are hiding under the bed, I give you my word.
The idea of vampires thirsting for blood is plain absurd.
Headless horsemen, hocus pocus and aliens, all nonsense.
You'll find you will not fall under a witch's spell.
You are not Snow White, nor am I a handsome prince,
But still a kiss. God bless. Goodnight.

Rhiah Doldersum (8)
Newport Community School, Barnstaple

My Cat Jerry

My cat Jerry is very lazy and fat
He sleeps all day long on my
Bedroom mat
He's my cat Jerry

He's grey and white
His eyes are bright
He's my cat Jerry

He chases mice around the house
They squeak a lot and run and run
And Jerry thinks it's a lot of fun
He's my cat Jerry

He chases me up the garden path
And attacks my feet
Just like a shark
He's *my cat Jerry!*

Hannah Bound (9)
Newport Community School, Barnstaple

The Sea

The sea is clear as crystals,
It brushes onto the shore.
The sea carries pebbles into the blue waters.

Creatures play in the sun all day,
Frisking, splashing and having fun.
The dolphins squeak to each other.

Under the blue depths seaweed dances,
The current tugs it and pulls its roots,
The slimy plant is home to some animals.

The sea at night crashes cliffs,
And finds shells.
Then rests like a blanket.
It glistens in the moonlight.

Beth Unstead (10)
Newport Community School, Barnstaple

Ilfracombe

We climbed up the hill
So steep and slimy;
When we got to the top
We said, 'Cor blimey!'
We turned around and looked at the sea,
And said, 'What a wonderful place this is to be!'
The waves, how they rumbled and tumbled,
The wind, how it roared with rage;
The rain was pouring down,
And Dad said, 'Hey, look at the town!'
The town looked like an underwater city
Alone and deserted, it's such a pity.
Dad said, 'It's time to go.'
And we said, 'Cheerio!'
And slid down the hill.
We got covered in mud
And landed with a thud!

Chloe Macree (8)
Newport Community School, Barnstaple

Girly Girls

Girls, girls, girls, I'm glad I'm a girl;
We like doing our hair
With ribbons and bows,
And most of all with curls and glitter.

Make-up, make-up, make-up,
How I love to make-up,
With lipstick and gloss,
Eye shadow and glitter.

Clothes, clothes, clothes,
I'm mad about clothes,
Jeans, tops,
Boots and shoes,
Leggings and skirts.

Hollie Wright (10)
Newport Community School, Barnstaple

The Poem I Didn't Write

I didn't know what to write this poem about.
So it made me scream and shout.

I lobbed my pencil at the wall.
It bounced away into the hall.

Leaning back on my chair I tipped.
That is when my trousers ripped.

They made a terrible tearing sound.
Then slowly tumbled to the ground.

My chair fell back, I bumped my head.
My mummy sent me up to bed.

So my poem I couldn't write.
That's all I have to say. Goodnight.

Timothy Chamings (10)
Newport Community School, Barnstaple

Rupert's Poem, Edition One

I enjoy football,
I enjoy football,
Football is fun,
I enjoy football.

I have big fields,
I have big fields,
There is a big red plane
Swooping through my fields.

I have big, brainy computers
And they do everything for me;
I have big brainy computers
And they do everything for me.

Rupert Beer (9)
Newport Community School, Barnstaple

The Wind

The wind flows like a blanket
It rushes through the air
The wind rattles the windows
Of the old house standing there

The wind has a frightening sound
Whistling around the garden
Blowing the leaves off the trees
Bare trees are left standing

The wind makes people dress up warm
Woolly hats, coats, scarves and gloves
I can't wait for summer to come.

Sydney Miles (9)
Newport Community School, Barnstaple

My Dad

My dad passed away.
He passed away on
Saturday 16th December.
His family dearly loved him,
But I loved him more because
I was a dad's girl and I always
Will be. But I can remember
Putting Dad's glasses on;
They were really big glasses.
I will never forget my dad,
Ian Charles Brice. I love
You, Dad, and I know you loved me.
Rest in peace.

Emma Brice (10)
Newport Community School, Barnstaple

Football Is Like . . .

Football is like . . . Acting
the pitch is my stage.

Football is like . . . Wrestling
the referee's my cage.

Football is like . . . Appointments
the wait is my free kick.

Football is like . . . Possessions
the pride's my hat-trick.

Aaron Barnes (11)
Newport Community School, Barnstaple

A Kitten

Catnapper
Milk lapper

Loud purrer
Long starer

Food taker
Fight faker

High leaper
Silent creeper.

Aimie Footman (10)
Newport Community School, Barnstaple

Whale

W is for water, the oceans of the world,
H is for hammerhead shark, not everyone's best friend;
A is for anemone, swaying with the tide,
L is for limpet, clinging to the rocks,
E is for electric eel, frightening creatures away.

Blake Ladley (10)
Newport Community School, Barnstaple

Horses

Standing in the stables
Bridles under their labels

Munching on their food
In a happy mood

Cantering your horse
Through a jumping course

Having a horse of your own
Or keeping one on loan

On the beach in the saddle
Taking the horses for a paddle.

Myah Field (11)
Newport Community School, Barnstaple

Angels

A is for angel up in the sky,
N is for new angels rising up high,
G is for God who created the world.
E is for everlasting faith which is in us all,
L is for love in the world all around.

Katie Ladley (11)
Newport Community School, Barnstaple

My Cat Blacky

My cat Blacky sleeps everywhere,
She sleeps in the sink in the bathroom,
She sleeps in the roasting dish on top of the cooker,
She sleeps in the tumble dryer full of clothes,
She sleeps on top of the printer in the living room,
You never know where she's going to sleep next!

Hannah Sutton (11)
Newport Community School, Barnstaple

Tennis

Tennis is my favourite game,
Winning a point is the aim.

Forehand is my favourite shot,
My volleys are the worst out of the lot.

The instructors are so cool,
They're the funniest of us all.

When I play with my dad,
Then I beat him he gets really mad.

I love to play a competitive match,
All the points I love to snatch.

At the end of the match,
I hold up my trophy in front of the crowd,
I am so very proud.

Alice Field (10)
Newport Community School, Barnstaple

Mr Jenkins

Early riser, speedy walker,
Goalie shooter,
Football lover,
Ball diver,
Probably a fab board rider,
Busy father,
Good listener,
Mr Jenkins,
My favourite teacher!

China-Blue Pascoe (10)
Newport Community School, Barnstaple

Football

I like football,
I know you will agree,
I run round the pitch,
As fast as I can be.

I am now getting tired,
With all the running around,
I know I need a rest
Or I will fall down;

I am now going to quit,
I cannot go on,
I am leaving the pitch,
Or I will get a stitch.

Liam Howells (8)
Newport Community School, Barnstaple

Crocodile

C reeping through the murky water.
R ipping and tearing through its prey.
O n the prowl all day long.
C reating fear among humans and animals.
O n the search for food in rivers and on land.
D estruction is its middle name.
I ntelligence is one of its many strengths,
L ying on top of the water lifeless, motionless.
E nergy conserving, the croc, a predator of the river.

Charlotte Rushton (11)
Newport Community School, Barnstaple

The Eagle

Bird of great power
Of both beauty and grace
Soars through the sky
Talons sharp, piercing screech
Swoops close to the ground
In search of its prey
Keen eyes scan the forest and fields all about
Noticing everything, nothing is safe
The hunter is hunting
Power, beauty and grace.

Gemma Wells (11)
Newport Community School, Barnstaple

Fluff The Rabbit

R unning, racing, jumping, hurling, rabbit goes to the food;
A lways bright and ready, sleeps all day and nibbles at night;
B ouncing around, no fear, happy and chomping is a rabbit's world;
B ringing joy to the owners for years, cute little face
   and two floppy ears;
I n his hutch he snuggles up tight, then he goes to sleep
   without fear of the night;
T reats are what rabbits want, though not good for them
   they make 'em jump!

Bradley Bell (10)
Newport Community School, Barnstaple

The Angry Shark

In the strong, shadowy waters
There lived an angry, anxious shark who wanted
To kill the hunters who wanted to kill him.
'Oh no!' whispered the shark, suddenly a net nearly fell on him.
Frightened the enormous shark swam away, fast as lightning.

Nicholas Raymond (7)
Newport Community School, Barnstaple

Football

Football's so fun,
Football's so great,
It's good to keep fit,
And makes you new mates!

Football's so cool,
It makes you fast,
You run up the wing,
And make a great pass!

Bradley Medhurst (10)
Newport Community School, Barnstaple

Who Am I?

Coffee drinker,
Biscuit eater,
Fun stopper,
Nit picker,
Loud shouter
Children scarer
Work giver
Child borer,
Advice sharer,
Child carer.

Jacob Harris (11)
Newport Community School, Barnstaple

The Cat

When I go hunting
I always catch a mouse
I take it to my house

A present for my family
They throw it away
I only wanted to play.

Luke Pincombe (7)
Newport Community School, Barnstaple

Summertime

In the summer waves splash and rivers flow,
In the summer flowers shine and people jump,
In the summer plants wave and trees bump,
In the summer water spills and cups smash,
In the summer fish wriggle and lions roar,
In the summer monkeys swing and elephants stomp,
In the summer snakes slide and leaves float,
In the summer boys talk and girls play,
In the summer frogs croak and men laugh,
In the summer bees buzz and butterflies bounce.

Lauren Smale (7)
Newport Community School, Barnstaple

When The Wind Blows!

When the wind blows trees mutter leaves flutter,
When the wind blows leaves flutter while we are working,
When the wind blows scarves fly away and coats try to take off,
When the wind blows hats come off heads so do scarves,
When the wind blows the grass looks like a green sea,
When the wind blows all you can hear is the wind howling and whistling,
When the wind blows trees rustle while we sing a song with the noise of the trees rustling in it.

Laura Phipps (8)
Newport Community School, Barnstaple

Spaghetti

Spaghetti, spaghetti you make a mess,
Spaghetti, spaghetti you're slithery,
Spaghetti, spaghetti I love you with cheese,
Spaghetti, spaghetti I can't have enough of you,
Spaghetti, spaghetti you are the best.

Emily Bale (7)
Newport Community School, Barnstaple

The Stormy Weather

The trees blew so strong that the branches snapped,
The leaves fell off the trees onto the ground;
The children were splashing in the puddles;
The rain was falling down heavily and the clouds were black;
Lightning was coming from the sky with the thunder;
The kids got their hats and scarves,
Gloves and coats on to keep them warm.
The storm got worse and worse.
The children went outside to play.

Shane Blackmore (7)
Newport Community School, Barnstaple

Butterflies

Butterflies, butterflies
Flutter by.
Butterflies, butterflies
Sniff flowers,
Their beautiful colours and shapes are so lovely.
Butterflies, butterflies
Have so delicate wings
And they are so fluffy and cute!

Katie Harris (8)
Newport Community School, Barnstaple

The Wind

The wind blows as fast, as fast as a galloping horse;
The wind is like crashing, jumping waves;
The wind is a like a howling, roaring fierce lion;
The wind is so blustery;
The wind whistles through the trees;
The wind is so biting and nipping to your ears.

Katie Shutt (8)
Newport Community School, Barnstaple

The Beach

The sea is sloshing on the beach,
Lots of surfers surfing in the waves.

Sunburnt tourists trying to cool down
Ice cream melting on their toes.

Children wearing scarves and hats,
And dogs paddling in the sea.

Lots of people having picnics,
Children playing beside a rock pool.

Building sandcastles and twisting cartwheels,
Flapping sails out to sea.

Searching for shells along the seashore,
The crabs are sliding to and fro.

Starfish sticking to the rocks,
Seaweed swishing in the sea.

Mila Maxwell (8)
Newport Community School, Barnstaple

Sunday Lunch

I love to munch
On my Sunday lunch;

I love my meat,
When it's been in the heat;

I love my roast
The most.

We sit round together,
I could eat this forever and ever!

Martha Cumiskey (8)
Newport Community School, Barnstaple

People

People are tall
People are small

People have big feet
People have little feet

People are crazy
People are lazy

People have long hair
People have short hair

People are old
People are young

No matter what
We are all the same.

Niamh Marshall (8)
Newport Community School, Barnstaple

Horses

Horses are cool
Horses are pretty
They live in the country
And not in the city.

Horses are big
Horses are small
Please be careful
You do not fall.

My favourite is Willow
She is the best
I love riding Willow
Until she must rest.

Hayley McDine (7)
Newport Community School, Barnstaple

My Favourite Things

Football is great,
Tennis is super,
Cheese is good,
Chocolate is better!

Snooker is brill,
Darts is terrific,
Pizza is magic,
Roasties are fab.

Drums are loud,
Hockey is fast,
Carrots are crunchy,
Peppers are perfect.

Bowling is best,
Swimming is special,
Salami is scrummy,
Ice cream is cool!

Max Kilham (8)
Newport Community School, Barnstaple

My Best Friend

My best friend is Chloe
Her hair colour is kind of snowy;
She is really very funny,
And she did once have a bunny.
She comes to my house quite a lot,
And we always seem to make a plot,
My best friend is Chloe,
Her hair colour is kind of snowy.

Jessica Foster (8)
Newport Community School, Barnstaple

My Blue Peter Badge

M y own Blue Peter badge.
Y ou can feel the bumpiness of the ship.

B ursting to open the letter.
L et everyone see it.
U sed with hammabeads
E xcited when I saw it.

P roud to have one.
E xpeditions that Blue Peter have been on.
T aken 5 months to make my hammabeads.
E xcellent models.
R elieved that I've got one at last.

B rilliant that I can touch one.
A mazing that I made it out of hammabeads.
D ad jealous that I've got one.
G reat, Blue Peter is based on a ship.
E xcellent pets.

Bethany Clarke (9)
Newport Community School, Barnstaple

At The Pet Shop

I went to the pet shop to get myself a dog,
They had no dogs so I looked for a frog,
I asked the owner for one of them,
He said he had none, so I asked for a hen,
The hens were all gone, it's not very funny,
I got a bit cross and asked for a bunny.
I bought a bunny,
It was so funny.

Jodee Stevens (7)
Newport Community School, Barnstaple

My Dog

My dog is lazy,
He gets really crazy,
And likes to dream in his sleep.

When he is fast
You can't see the grass;
And he leaves a trail of fire.

He likes to eat cheese,
And sometimes eats leaves,
And has a roast on Sunday.

He doesn't like people,
His bark is quite lethal,
And he growls at every stranger he sees.

He barks at a knock on the door,
He'll run and lie on the floor,
And growl as much as he can.

Jamie Smith (10)
Newport Community School, Barnstaple

Dr Who

My favourite telly show
It has to be
'Dr Who!' All the
Monsters amaze me.
They have strange faces
And funny names.
Sometimes you see
Dr Who games.
Maybe I could be the Doctor,
And not go to school.
That would be cool!

Tommy Hirst (7)
Newport Community School, Barnstaple

The Beach

As I see the waves drifting along the sand
I can feel some sprinkles of water on my hand.

As I see the seagulls flying to the east,
My legs sink into the sand, getting weaker and weaker.

As I hear the waves crashing on the rocks
I drop all the shells that I've got.

As my eyes melt into the sun
The waves chase me as I run.

As I slowly walk on the bumpy stones
They slide into the sandals that I own.

As I run out into the sea
All the waves go calm, I agree.

When I power walk out of the water to get a towel
From the south I hear a howl.

Serena Barrow (9)
Newport Community School, Barnstaple

Untitled

I went to the poet camp
I was the poet champ;
Now it's hard to stop making rhymes,
I must have tried
About a thousand times.
When I was there
I met Tony Blair
Or was it the mayor?
He was tall
With curly hair.

Abigail Brock (9)
Newport Community School, Barnstaple

My Dog Diesel

My dog, Diesel, has a very wet nose
And a very waggy tail
That only wags when he is happy.
When he is sad his eyes will go all droopy
And he will come and put his head on your lap,
Hoping that you will stroke him.
When Diesel gets in the bath
He will splash the whole bathroom,
And he will get told off by Daddy.
Then, when he has had his bath
He will go and lie down
By the fire and get dry.
When he has got dirty he will be happy again,
And he will want to go out in the garden
And play with you, and he will get really rough.
When you call him in he won't want to come
And he will stay out there.

Chloe Medhurst (9)
Newport Community School, Barnstaple

Snooker

Cue chalked,
Balls crash,
Aim, fire,
Balls spin,
Pockets fill,
Balls jump,
Points added,
Balls travel,
Black potted,
Snooker's fun!

Dean Bale (9)
Newport Community School, Barnstaple

The Storm

Gales blowing,
Wind howling,
Rooftops off,
Trees crashing to the ground,
Huge waves roaming,
Rivers flowing,
Roads flooded,
Cars skidding,
Drivers crashing,
It's cold,
People freezing,
Then the sun comes out.

Dale Leach (9)
Newport Community School, Barnstaple

Fruit

Fruit is sweet,
It is colourful
And very bright;
It is good for you
So take a bite.
Strawberries, grapes, bananas
Are just a few to chew.
Apples and plums
Are really great too.
But the best by far
Is the satsuma.

Rhiannon Smith (9)
Newport Community School, Barnstaple

Surfing

On a weekend
We go to the sea
We love to go surfing
Mum, Dad and me

When going surfing
I jump on my board
For the sand and the sea
I bless the Lord

Getting on the board
Catching that wave
I have to admit
I'm its slave

Once I have started
I'm totally in
It's like I'm growing
A human fish fin.

Chandler Tregaskes (10)
Newport Community School, Barnstaple

Bath Time

When I'm in my bubble bath,
I like to stir up more.
Most of the suds go in my eyes,
The rest go on the floor.

Water is good for your skin,
It gets you nice and clean,
It makes my skin all wrinkly,
It's good to have hygiene.

And when I splash them hard enough,
They pop and disappear.
Then my bath time's over,
I've made the water clear.

Tayler Horn (10)
Newport Community School, Barnstaple

Pink, Pink, I Love Pink

Pink, pink, I love pink,
Fluffy hearts and candyfloss.
Pink, pink, I love pink,
Soft cushions and bed socks;
Pink, pink, I love pink,
Twinkling lights and cherry drops;
Pink, pink, I love pink,
Dresses, shoes and shiny tops,
Pink, pink, I love pink,
There are lots of colours -
But what do you think of?
Pink!

Grace Sanders (8)
Newport Community School, Barnstaple

When I Leave School

When I leave school I want to be a superstar,
Driving in my fancy car!

When I leave school I want to be a vet,
Looking after all my pets!

When I leave school I want to be a superhero,
Shooting through all the stars!

When I leave school I want to be a chef,
Cooking up, all my best!

When I leave school I want to be a spy,
Spying, spying high up in the sky!

When I leave school I want to be a . . .

Chloe Mundell (9)
Newport Community School, Barnstaple

My Season Poem

In spring I go on
Easter egg hunts around
The garden. In the spring
The bunnies pop their heads
Out of their holes.

In the summer it's hot
And sticky. In the summer
We go on holiday with our
Family. In summer we wear
Our T-shirts and shorts.

In autumn it's cold and windy.
The wind blows and the leaves fall
Gracefully to the ground. We wrap up
Snug in our hats and scarves.

In winter it's bitterly
Cold and very miserable.
But in winter we have
Christmas time and
Christmas is a chance
For families to be together.

Phoebe Pethick (9)
Newport Community School, Barnstaple

Why Does Everyone Love Elephants?

You're big and gentle with flapping ears
You trumpet with your trunk so everyone hears
Your memory never lets you down
Your colour is grey and it is not brown
You can even spout water from your incredible nose
When you use it, it could be mistaken for a hose
That's why everyone loves elephants.

Emer O'Driscoll-Paton (9)
Newport Community School, Barnstaple

My Cat, Zac

I have a cat called Zac,
He likes to sit on my lap;
He's getting rather old,
That, I have been told.
He curls up in his bed.
After being well fed.
When you stroke his fur
He starts to purr.
He can jump very high,
But not to the sky!
He licks his toes,
And has a wet nose.
When Zac catches a mouse
He brings it into the house,
And Mum goes totally mad
Because she thinks it's really bad.
She throws the mouse away
And Zac carries on to play,
And that's the end of his day.

Lee Barnes (9)
Newport Community School, Barnstaple

Swimming

S wimming is a sport
W hich makes you healthy,
I love swimming and
M aking a splash as I dive.
M um's shivering at the edge,
I nfants flapping, trying to swim and
N ever giving up.
G reat fun for everyone!

Jennifer Proctor (9)
Newport Community School, Barnstaple

Fishing Day

I like fishing, catching fish in the sea;
Sometimes my daddy comes fishing with me;
I eat all the sandwiches, I sometimes eat the bait!
I'll even eat my daddy's if I cannot wait.
I sit all day, watching my float
Bobbing up and down like a tiny little boat.
I watch the fish jumping up and down,
Catching the bait with their little mouths.
I reel in my line and pack it all away.
I really wanted to stay for the rest of the day!

Joseph Freeman (9)
Newport Community School, Barnstaple

Rugby

I love rugby!
It's one of my favourite sports
Because I get all muddy
On my nice clean shorts;
When I'm cold, wet and hungry
I sometimes want to cry,
But it makes me feel better
When I score the winning try!

Alfie Pennyfield (9)
Newport Community School, Barnstaple

Sea Creatures

Whales sing and flap their fins,
Whales blow a water spout;
Dolphins chatter as they
Leap in and out;
In the big blue sea.

Joseph Micklewright (9)
Newport Community School, Barnstaple

Alphabet Animals

A is for an alligator with his big white teeth
B is for a bunny that will chomp on a leaf
C is for a crocodile that will swim down the Nile
D is for a dolphin that will swim a mile.
E is for elephant that is big and strong
F is for a frog that will hop along
G is for giraffe that will gaze into the sky
H is for hippo that will give a big sigh
I is for insects that are small creepy bugs
J is for jellyfish that has no blood
K is for kangaroo with its great big hop
L is for lion that has a mane like a mop
M is for mouse that loves to eat cheese
N is for narwhal, the whale from the icy seas
O is for octopus that has no scales
P is for pony that swishes its tail
Q is for quetzal, a small bird that eats frogs
R is for rabbit that hops over logs
S is for shark that swims in the sea
T is for tiger that would like to eat me
U is for uakari, a monkey which is fairly small
V is for vicuna, a camel that doesn't have a hump at all
W is for worm that loves the ground
X is for X-ray fish that will lurk around
Y is for yellow-bellied snake that frightens me
Z is for zebra that eats leaves from a tree.

Jessica Lobb (10)
Newport Community School, Barnstaple

My Dream Came True

Before I went to Disney I hoped
We would go on a safari;
When we arrived at the park
Before I knew it crocodiles were footsteps away,
Zebras were munching like mad,
Cheetahs were lazing about,
Elephants tooting their trunks
And giraffes showing off their long necks.
After the safari I felt incredible
Because I love animals.
Safaris show animals
And so my dream came true!

Lewis Walker (9)
Newport Community School, Barnstaple

I Like Coconut

I like the taste of coconut
Cracking in my crunch

I like the smell of coconut
Wafting in the wind

I like the feel of coconut
Tickling my tongue

I like the sound of coconut
Shaking in its shell

I like the sight of coconut
All brown and burnt by the sun.

Erik Wilson (9) & Benjamin Harvey (7)
Newton Ferrers CE Primary School, Plymouth

Redcurrants

I like redcurrants

I like the taste of redcurrants
Fizzing on my tingling tongue

I like the smell of redcurrants
All sweet on my nutty nose

I like the feel of shiny redcurrants
Hard in my hand

I like the sound of redcurrants
Squidging and echoing in my ear

I like the sight of redcurrants
Glowing rosy, ruby-red.

Nathan King, Harry Guy (8) & Imogen Tarran (9)
Newton Ferrers CE Primary School, Plymouth

Strawberries

I like strawberries

I like the taste of strawberries
Melting my mouth

I like the smell of strawberry juice
Juggling in my mouth

I like the feel of smooth strawberries
Rubbing on my hands

I like the sound of strawberries
Squeezing strawberry juice

I like the sight of strawberries
Shimmering in the sun
I like strawberries.

Anna Barnett & Molly Finch (8)
Newton Ferrers CE Primary School, Plymouth

The Demontooth
(Based on 'The Jabberwocky' by Lewis Carroll)

'Twas bleak, and the slithey fogs
Did gyre and gimble in the swamp;
All mimsy were the flutterbys,
And the lambocks were grave.

'Beware the Demontooth, my friend!
The tail that crushes the teeth tear!
Beware the Spirit Walker and shun
The Death Seeker.

He took his flob axe in his hand:
Long time the meatchay foe he sought
So rested by the claw tree.
And stood a while and thought.

And as in dreeday through he stood,
The Demontooth, with eyes of flame,
Came tearing through the chader tree,
And slobbering as it came!

One, two! One, two and through and through,
The flob axe went snicker-snack!
He left it mangled and with its talon
He went galumphing back.

'And hast thou slain the Demontooth?
Come to my arms my beamish boy
O frabjous day! Oh chimpay! Chimpay!'
He chortled in his joy.

'Twas bleak, and the slithey fogs
Did gyre and gimble in the swamp;
All mimsy were the flutterbys,
And the tambocks were grave.

Emily Vyain (10)
Newton Ferrers CE Primary School, Plymouth

The Bug Bug
(Based on 'The Jabberwocky' by Lewis Carroll)

'Twas Sunday, and the Nellies
Did gyre and gimble in the mountains;
All mimsy were the Berties,
In the cave.

'Beware the Bug Bug, my friend!
The arms that sting, the mouth that cracks!
Beware the Nug Nug and shun
The Ugevil.'

He took his sharp axe in hand:
Long time the Bug Bug foe he sought -
So rested he by the tree
And stood a while in thought.

And as in tring bring thought he stood,
The Bug Bug, with eyes of flame,
Came sugbugnuging through the woods,
And singing as it came!

One, two! One, two! And through and through
The axe went snicker-snack!
He left it dead, and with its head
He went galumphing back.

'And hast thou slain the Bug Bug?
Come to my arms, my beamish boy!
O frabjous day! Bi bi bi! Bi bi bi!'
He chortled in his joy.

'Twas Sunday, and the Nellies
Did gyre and gimble in the mountains;
All mimsy were the Berties,
In the cave.

Benjamin King (10)
Newton Ferrers CE Primary School, Plymouth

The Demontooth
(Based on 'The Jabberwocky' by Lewis Carroll)

'Twas bleak, and the slithey Fogs
Did gyre and gimble in the swamp;
All mimsy were the Flutterbys,
And the tambocks were grave.

'Beware the Demontooth, my friend!
The tail that crushes the teeth tear!
Beware the spirit Walker and shun
The Death Speaker.

He took his flob axe in hand:
Long time the meatchay foe he sought -
So rested by the claw trees.
And stood a while in thought.

And as in dreeday thought he stood,
The Demontooth came
Tearing through the chader tree,
And slobbering as it came!

One, two! One, two! And through and through,
The flob axe went snicker-snack!
He left it mangled and with its talon
He went galumphing back.

'And hast thou slain the Demontooth?
Come to my arms my beamish boy
O frabjous day! Oh chimpay! Chimpay!'
He chortled in his joy.

'Twas bleak, and the slithey fogs
Did gyre and gimble in the swamp;
All mimsy were the flutterbys,
And the tambocks were grave.

Bryony Lawes (10)
Newton Ferrers CE Primary School, Plymouth

Pineapple

I like pineapple

I like the taste of pineapple
Tingling on my tongue

I like the smell of pineapple
Nuzzling up my nose

I like the feel of pineapple
Prickling all of my palm

I like the sound of pineapple
Squelching and splashing when it is sawn

I like the sight of pineapple
Like an exotic African hat in the circus.

Tanya Pearson & James Wall (9)
Newton Ferrers CE Primary School, Plymouth

Coconut

I like coconut

I like the taste of coconut
Munching in my mouth

I like the smell of coconut
Coming up my nose

I like the feel of coconut
Its bristles, hairy scrunching in my hand

I like the sound of coconut milk
Drifting in its shell

I like the sight of coconut
Crushing on a cliff.

Jack Lake & Fergus Carruthers (8)
Newton Ferrers CE Primary School, Plymouth

Pineapple

I like pineapple

I like the taste of pineapple
Melting in my mouth

I like the smell of pineapple
Nuzzling up my nose

I like the feel of pineapple
Scratching my fingers

I like the sound of pineapple
Crunching in my mouth

I like the sight of pineapple
Glowing in the dark.

Sophie Hartley (8) & Juliet Hepburn (9)
Newton Ferrers CE Primary School, Plymouth

Coconut

I like coconut

I like the taste of coconut
Slurping in my mouth

I like the smell of coconut
In a glass

I like the feel of smooth coconut
Fuzzy hairs tickling my fingers

I like the sound of coconut milk
Splashing inside the coconut

I like the sight of coconut
Hanging from a tree.

Georgina McCartney (8) & Harry Honeywill (7)
Newton Ferrers CE Primary School, Plymouth

Strawberries

I like strawberries

I like the taste of strawberries
Squelching in my mouth

I like the smell of strawberries
Sweet in my sniff

I like the feel of smooth strawberries
Bumpy in my hand

I like the sound of strawberries
Squirting on my lips

I like the sight of strawberries
Raging red hearts in their box.

Chloe Bruniges & Elodie Hind (7)
Newton Ferrers CE Primary School, Plymouth

The Basins

The river is calm, the river is relaxing,
It keeps me happy all day and night,
The tree is rough, the tree is bumpy and while I'm asleep
the wind blows it softly.
The grass is green, the grass is shiny and the dewdrops
are making it shimmer as the sun beats down.
While I'm watching this happen it makes me feel very contented.

Emily Buttle (9)
Rockwell Green CE Primary School, Rockwell Green

A Frosty Journey

The river was flowing freezing, frosty and cold.
With the coldness rushing past my face.

The trees rushing really fast,
Wind blowing everywhere,
The crazy tree rustling past my hair.

The tree feels rough, bumpy and hard,
The dog barking because it's really angry,
Running as fast as it can.

The old rusty bridge not stable anymore,
Well, the next time that someone walks on it,
It might collapse.

The green oak tree nearly as tall as the sky,
Lots of branches hanging off, rough and barky.

My nose as cold as an icicle, as shivery as the wind,
A cold icicle on a windowpane, trying to break off
Shivery, cold, red and freezing.

The duck as soft as a feather flapping its wings,
Ducking its head in the water, so beautiful,
Swimming in the water so smooth soft and fluffy.

Lauren Fyfe (8)
Rockwell Green CE Primary School, Rockwell Green

My Journey

On the journey, on the journey,
I saw the river, rustling and gusting by.

On the journey, on the journey,
I saw a dog, barking and howling while he runs.

On the journey, on the journey,
I saw the dew, shimmering and gleaming in the sun.

On the journey, on the journey,
I saw the reflections of trees, dark and ghostly in the water.

On the journey, on the journey,
I saw a duck, bobbing, bobbing, bobbing on the pond.

On the journey, on the journey,
I saw the trees, swaying and swinging.

After the journey, after the journey,
I was cosy in the comfort of my house.

Ryan Pidgeon (9)
Rockwell Green CE Primary School, Rockwell Green

A Frosty Journey

Gentle river, bubbles trickling, clear, reflecting, frothing too.
Icy air blowing (wear your mittens) chills run down your spine.
Hear the birds sing in the distance.
The water rippling through grey pebbles.
Dogs are barking, *woof, woof, woof.*
Rough tree bark with knobs and cracks.
Old with muddy moss, brambles and thorns
Surround the tree, crumbling tough and tall.

Brown grass, green grass,
Glittering dew drops, sparkling, overgrown.
A moorhen comes.

Now I am much too cold, but there's no place like home.

Hannah Druce (8)
Rockwell Green CE Primary School, Rockwell Green

My Freezing Journey

Down by the basins
There's a rushing, running, rippling river.
There is a mix of nice smelling plants,
But most of all it is freezing, freezing, freezing my toes.
Further on there is a dog,
Wagging, wagging, wagging his tail,
Freezing cold hands numb, frozen, cold as ice,
My nose is red, can't feel it, trees curling, frizzling, hugging.
Then I come across geese, swimming, swimming in the pond,
There are ducks swimming with the geese.
My hands are so cold I can't write.
The wind is blowing badly through my hair,
The trees have squirrels jumping tree by tree.
The dog is soaked, soaked, soaked top to bottom,
Further on I come across a train going bumpy, rattling over the track,
The train was making a noise,
A noise that goes *'Chuka, chuka, chuka, choo.'*
I can see the sun reflecting in the flowing river,
I can see leaves blowing with the breeze in the trees.
I can hear the motorway in the background,
Cars going along with the wind.
Then I carry on walking and there is a broken fence,
A person walking, walking her dog,
At the end of the basins there is a pond
With lilies floating, floating on the pond,
Making me want to float away, float away, float away.

Lucy May (10)
Rockwell Green CE Primary School, Rockwell Green

A Frosty Morning

On a frosty morning when all is quiet,
Magical reflections glisten in the water,
You can hear the faint sound of the water rippling over the stones,
You can see the white snow settling on the ground.

Kieran Martin (8)
Rockwell Green CE Primary School, Rockwell Green

The Winter Walk

The dog is running, barking, laying, sitting.
The tree is waving, swishing, swashing.
The water is rushing, wishing, swishing.
The birds are singing, tingling, ringing.
I see dew on the grass trickling
Twinkling, sparkling, shimmering.
The rocks in the water rough and smooth.
The ducks in the water swimming and quacking.
My nose is cold, runny, numb, so cold I can't feel a thing.
The leaves are dead, yellow, brown, small, big.
My ears are cold, ice-cold.
The sun shining, hitting the grass and making it glimmer, shine.
The clouds white as snow with the sun coming through the clouds.
The gate was ice-cold the metal was as hard as a tree trunk.
The tree was bending over, twisting, twirling, waving
                          in the gentle breeze.
The train makes a big noise when it beeps the big horn.
The air is blowing, crisp, whooshing ice-cold as it goes past.
The bridge is stony hard, ice-cold.
My hands froze when I touched it, my hands turned numb.

Reanna Anderson (10)
Rockwell Green CE Primary School, Rockwell Green

Basins

The gentle flowing river is flowing down the stream.
The trees are rustling, rustling, rustling, rustling.
The ducks are quacking, quacking, quacking.

The dew is glossy on the grass in the sunlight
My fingers are numb and cold and blue,
I cross the old bridge with a crunch, crunch, crunch!
A squirrel is jumping from tree to tree to tree.

Bethany Lowman (8)
Rockwell Green CE Primary School, Rockwell Green

A Winter Walk

There's a tree that's making a reflection,
Over the river, fresh and clear,
A big brown dog waggling his tail
I can hear birds almost like I can see them.
Another tree that is rough, hanging over the water
Filled up with pebbles, yellow and mouldy sits in the water.
I see the sun high up in the sky feeling the warmth on my face,
My nose is red and cold,
The air is fresh and bitter,
I feel not like before
I don't like being cold but it's worth it
My hair is blowing, blowing through the air.
The tree looks old, the oldest I have ever seen.
I can't believe my eyes, it looks so green.
The metal gate looks dented in, I can't believe my eyes!
It needs to be fixed again.
The grass is so slippery, icy too!
You need to be careful you might slip too!
My hands are frozen, I cannot move them at all.
Be careful! You need to keep them warm!

Rebecca White (9)
Rockwell Green CE Primary School, Rockwell Green

A Frosty Journey

Trees standing still, chunky, bumpy and rough,
Freezing hands, frosty air, magnificently cold,
A great pebble beach, an excited dog, bouncing through the grass,
Ducks talking to each other in their own language,
Stream water calmly floating by, muddy, clear, muddy, clear
Frost sitting on the grass shining, as the sun's rays bounce
                                                    off the blades.

Mitchell Sims (10)
Rockwell Green CE Primary School, Rockwell Green

A Frosty Cold Journey

The river is running, running so fast.
The pebbles on the bottom shining at last,
The tree is so big, so brown and so old,
Its bark is so rough, lumpy and cold.
I can hear the cars on the motorway,
The dogs are barking as loud as they can,
The best sound of all is the birds humming their songs,
The bush so tall and so spiky,
The yellowy brown colour is not a nice sight.
The dew on the grass so wet, and so green.
The shining is amazing to me, all there is left for me to say
Is the hot warm sun is out that day
I know it sounds odd but I'm telling the truth.

Ben Ellins (8)
Rockwell Green CE Primary School, Rockwell Green

A Magical Journey

Rivers glistening, flowing, rushing,
The trees felt old, cold and bold,
Bushes were rough and spiky like
Electric volts tickling my feet,
Dogs were barking, barking, barking.
My nose felt cold, pink, freezing,
Ducks made me feel warm, hot or cold,
The grass made a whistling noise through my ear,
And the motorway made a buzz, buzz,
Buzzing noise like a bee passing by.
The bridge made a knock, knock, knocking noise,
The sun was warm and made me happy again.

Owen Binding (10)
Rockwell Green CE Primary School, Rockwell Green

A Journey For Me

Rushing river, side to side, crashing off the walls and silt flowing into the
river and then settling, settling down on the bed.
Over the gleaming grassy hill with the tree-lined view,
A dog wagging its tail, soggy, sloshy too.
A tree bent over like a hunched back man
twisting, twirling in the wind, a gate squawking like a bird
and it's the most uncomfortable sound I've ever heard.
The water goes over and past the pebble beach, cleaning
them as nice and shiny as can be, my nose is cold like when you
spray water from a hose - shiver, shake, achoo.
A bird flying, swooping in the air, singing a lovely song.
An oak tree old, swishing and swaying with green and brown mould.
A lake with a duck swimming with its friends and then sitting in its nest.

Georgia Dodden (9)
Rockwell Green CE Primary School, Rockwell Green

Frogs

Frogs come in many colours
It's really hard to tell,
Who is who and what is what,
But there's one stuck down the well.

Some are *big*.
Some are small.
Some don't move much at all.

Some jump high.
Some croak low.
Tadpoles don't do that so *grow*.

Frogs come in many colours,
It's really hard to tell,
But you know who's who and what's what,
Including the one down the well.

Abby Partridge (11)
Rockwell Green CE Primary School, Rockwell Green

A Cold And Frosty Morning

A cold breeze smacks my face,
I see the river running at a steady pace,
The crystal-clear water shining in the sun,
I know the spring has begun.
I see a pretty girl with a camera; silver.
I sniff the air, what a clean smell,
An oak tree high bare of leaves, its massive
branches swimming in the breeze,
The morning sun makes the dew-covered grass shimmer.
My hands are cold, my nose is blue,
The morning birds are singing too,
I look up, I see wispy white clouds
With a background of clear blue sky,
I close my eyes and listen, I hear the
humming of the motorway.
There are Canadian geese floating gently
on the water's surface, and the reflections
of trees in the water look like dark soldiers.
Soldiers sleeping in the calm water's bed.

Benedict Monteiro (8)
Rockwell Green CE Primary School, Rockwell Green

A Winter Walk

I can see water running under me, muddy, muddy water,
I see fish in the muddy, muddy water.
Going further downstream, changing to clean, clean water.
I see a duck in the pond swimming in the water,
I wonder what they feel like in the water,
They must be cold in the winter -
The icy wind freezing the water.

I hear a train on the track making a clunk, clunk sound.
The engine zooming by all the ducks.
Frosty trees, the ones I can see,
The ones I can touch - with my warm hands.

Matthew Barr (9)
Rockwell Green CE Primary School, Rockwell Green

My Journey

The pebbles make a wavy pebble beach with a curling sound,
The sound of the river with stones bumping in the water
makes the river go lumpy and swirly,
My hands are frozen, like an ice cube; it's gone numb and cold,
The stones in the rushing river gush down the lane of the river water,
If you are quiet you can hear birds singing and motorway cars zooming
past on the road,
The trees are old from years of standing there. Its colour green
and brown with moss wet and soggy,
The rocky river sounds like a waterfall splashing,
The pond is still but the ducks are swirling, making it move,
I hear a dog barking by the dog path, barking, barking, barking!

Reegan Scotcher (9)
Rockwell Green CE Primary School, Rockwell Green

Nature

It is beautiful when you see the trees,
the flowers, the leaves, trees swaying and playing.
The sky is blue and clear, hedges still and stiff in the cold air,
Pebbles clinging and banging in the lazy stream,
sparkling grass shining and glowing bright green.
My cold shivering hands picked up gold leaves.
Frosty grass, frosty trees - I love nature,
it makes my heart bang and drum.
The sun gleaming on my face.
Cold stingy air, the numb air all around me.
I feel my knees in the wavy grass - blowing in the wind,
the whistling sound in the background taking me far,
far away in a path of mist.

Ashleigh Dodden (9)
Rockwell Green CE Primary School, Rockwell Green

Safari

Leaping gazelles dance,
Flying higher than the rest,
Showing off to their mates.

Laughing and cackling,
Over a rotting carcass,
Hyenas hunting.

Heavy as a whale,
The elephant means no harm,
Will protect its young.

Grey slippery skin,
Hippopotamus is big,
Very dangerous.

Stripy black and white,
Blending in with the dry grass,
The zebra is calm.

Soaring and flying,
The scavenger of the air,
The vulture swoops down.

George Green (10)
Rockwell Green CE Primary School, Rockwell Green

Fear

Fear is like black fog,
As it spikes people in the back,
Fear smells like blood,
Dripping, dripping, dripping,
Getting more shivery,
As the fear more tense,
Fear sounds like thunder and lightning
Crackling in the sky.

Chelsea Baker (11)
Rockwell Green CE Primary School, Rockwell Green

I Wanna Be A Racing Driver

I wanna be a racing driver,
I wanna be the one survivor,
I wanna be a drifting slider,
I don't wanna be caught with a cheating colider,
I wanna be a racing driver,

I wanna be a racing driver,
I wanna be faster than a circuit rider,
I wanna be a comer diver,
I will, I'll bet you a fiver,
OK you get the idea,
I wanna be a racing driver.

I wanna be a racing driver,
I wanna be a wheel spinner,
I wanna be a gear changer,
I wanna beat the contender,
I wanna be a championship winner,
I wanna be a racing driver!

Danny Morison & William Lane (10)
Rockwell Green CE Primary School, Rockwell Green

I Wanna Be A Pop Star

I wanna be a pop star,
I wanna own a bar,
I wanna dance on the floor,
I wanna sing some more
I wanna be a pop star
I wanna be with my grandma
When I sing
I wanna have an amazing bling
I wanna drive a cool car
I wanna get rid of my scar
I just wanna be a pretty
Super, pop star!

Sharnie Diston (10)
Rockwell Green CE Primary School, Rockwell Green

The Old Tree

It sways in the breeze from the fresh morning air,
It glistens and sparkles, lying in the cold frost
It feels like elephant skin,
Now the day is going to begin!

It sways in the breeze from the fresh midday air,
It remembers the people that have past,
How many branches gone? I don't know,
But I'm sure a few more will go.

It sways in the breeze from the fresh evening air,
It calms its branches as a dog tiptoes past,
It watches the sun and moon play chase,
It definitely wins the life-time race.

It sways in the breeze from the fresh night air,
It stands and waits for the morning to come,
Waiting there for the bright day sun.
Now that today is done!

A brand new day begins.

Molly Redstone (11)
Rockwell Green CE Primary School, Rockwell Green

The Big Old Tree

It sways in the breeze of the morning air,
The old tree, an old man in the past it has seen.
In the future you don't know what will become of that old tree.
It has been climbed on and wrecked but still it keeps going.

The wind blows so hard that it sways in the breeze
Daytime air wondering what will happen.

Rebecca Whyte (10)
Rockwell Green CE Primary School, Rockwell Green

Seasons - Haikus

Spring flowers blooming,
The ground comes to life, growing
Beautiful flowers.

Summer's hot, drying
Up all the ground, people lay
On a mat, they burn.

Autumn leaves fall down,
Leaving the ground covered in
Browns, golds, yellow leaves.

Winter's cold, snow starts
To fall, Christmas comes on the
Twenty-fifth, presents!

Jordan Webber (10)
Rockwell Green CE Primary School, Rockwell Green

The Old Man

Here stands the massive oak tree,
An old man, looking,
Just sitting there alone,
All on his own.

The bumps are like his eyes,
The creased bark is like his wrinkled skin,
In the summer he has hair,
But in the winter he is bare.

He has sweet acorns that grow in the spring,
And they fall off in the autumn,
He has been there for hundreds of years,
But on his knobbly face, we never found his ears.

Miriam Nadim (10)
Rockwell Green CE Primary School, Rockwell Green

I Wanna Be A Singer

I wanna be a singer
I wanna date a footballer,
I wanna drive a sports car,
I wanna have my own bar,
I wanna say goodbye to bills,
I wanna live in Beverley Hills,
I wanna be a singer,
I wanna have my name in lights,
I wanna go on lots of flights,
I wanna have lots of pets,
I wanna own private jets,
I wanna be a singer,
I wanna have loads of money,
I wanna live somewhere sunny,
I wanna sing in Hollywood,
I wanna go to Bollywood,
I wanna be the best,
I wanna be better than the rest,
I wanna be a singer.

Georgina Couzens (10)
Rockwell Green CE Primary School, Rockwell Green

The Old Oak Tree

The old oak tree is still standing strong
After all these years seeing so much
Children still climb on his branches long
He's seen them grow up to adults
Yet still they see him touch.

Ben Ware (10)
Rockwell Green CE Primary School, Rockwell Green

Lonely Swans

Two lonely swans gliding
across the frosty lake.
Silently the white snow
falls hour upon hour they
get colder and colder.
They find shelter under
an old frosty tree that
looks like an old man sitting
on the edge of the lake.
They blink the cold snow
flakes out of their eyes
as the snow falls through
the old branches of the trees.

Harriet Cornall (10)
Rockwell Green CE Primary School, Rockwell Green

My Pony And I

Over the fields and far away, my pony and I go out to play,
Monty's a chestnut, only six,
He shakes his head and rarely kicks,
He jumps beautifully over a wooden rail,
And lets me brush his golden tail,
I love him and he loves me,
Together we live in perfect harmony,
Over the fields and far away, my pony and I go out to play.

Connie Buttle (10)
Rockwell Green CE Primary School, Rockwell Green

The Old Oak Tree

The old oak spreads its leaves higher than the stars.
It's old and bare in the winter but in the summer it
blooms with leaves of green.

It's an old man with rough and tough old skin with bumps
and lumps of every sort.
With cobwebs and spiders on every arm.
It's full of memories and wonders of World Wars and new inventions.

In the autumn its leaves turn fire-red, flame-orange and golden-brown.
They swerve and turn in the wind as the tree moans and groans
                                                        and sways.
Old and tired now, standing alone in a field far away.

Rhiannon Sampson (10)
Rockwell Green CE Primary School, Rockwell Green

Love

Love
What is love?
Is it happiness
Or a peaceful white dove?
Could it be friendship and passion,
Laughter and compassion?
Why?
Why do we love?
For pleasure and desire
To keep our heart's fire burning,
For love it is yearning,
Calling out for adoration.
Love.

Samuel Buttle (11)
Rockwell Green CE Primary School, Rockwell Green

I Wanna Be A Football Star

I wanna be a football star,
I wanna drive a flashy car,
I wanna own a flashy bar,
I wanna be a football star.

I wanna be a football star,
I wanna move to Barcelona,
I want to play against Wayne Rooney,
I wanna be a football star.

I wanna be a football star,
I wanna be number one,
I wanna have lots of money,
I wanna be a football star.

I wanna be a football star,
I wanna win every cup,
I wanna be the top goal scorer,
I wanna be a football star.

Jake Penson (11)
Rockwell Green CE Primary School, Rockwell Green

Winter

The grass is a soft, frosty white,
After a long, cold, freezing night,
Glazed with a thick layer of crisp ice,
The pond is glistening, calming and nice,
Standing still the old oak tree,
Has the face of an old man living in there,
The park is a soft, frosty white,
After a long, cold, freezing night.

Abigail Carter (11)
Rockwell Green CE Primary School, Rockwell Green

Daylight Saving

Why do I play through the night
And sleep through the day?
Am I the opposite
Different to the rest?
I don't know why
Just ask the rest
I'm not scared
It's kinda fun
But I ask myself
Am I human
Or am I not?

Harry Mackenzie (10)
Rockwell Green CE Primary School, Rockwell Green

The Old Tree

It sways in the breeze of the daytime air
Waving side to side
Like an old person
Who lives in the past years

It sways in the breeze of the midnight air
Waving side to side
With badgers watching as they sniffle by.

Shannon Isaacs (9)
Rockwell Green CE Primary School, Rockwell Green

Extinction

Animals are the best for me,
Running, climbing, roaming free.
Giraffe, wild cats and boar,
Elephant, monkeys and many more.

If we destroy any more homes,
The animals won't be free to roam.
In a couple of years some won't be here,
And that's what I dread to fear.

Everyone needs to do their thing,
So whales and birds can continue to sing.
Don't take away their natural abode
Or there will be no animals when we grow old.

Kiera Chard (10)
Rockwell Green CE Primary School, Rockwell Green

Early Morning

Early morning sun peeping through the sky,
And the trees reaching for a fly.

Hard frozen mud like setting ice cream,
A blushing fountain about to scream.

Lumps and bumps of famous faces,
As the sun comes out the frost packs its cases.

Megan Dobson (11)
Rockwell Green CE Primary School, Rockwell Green

Global Warming

Sun beating
Earth heating
Ice melting
Seas rising
Ozone breaking
Trees burning
Land shrinking
Weather changing

Stop it now!

Recycling
Stop driving
No binning
Re-using
No flying
Stop burning
Start walking
Help animals
Save water
Turn lights off

Help!
Save our world!

Jack Trevail (11)
Threemilestone School, Truro

The Earth's Fall Down

The world we live in
Is getting hot,
Motorcars
We use them a lot.

Electricity just
Isn't helping
Greenhouse gases
Keep increasing

Weather cold,
Weather hot,
We are getting rid
Of what we should not

We are people
We roam the Earth
For the kids
Who have just had birth

We should make
A better Earth
For when they
Are roaming the turf.

Fergus Laity (11)
Threemilestone School, Truro

Man's Supreme Vanity

The sun's blazing, it's getting hot
All the cars aren't helping a lot
Life is something we have to think about
Doom will come without a doubt
If we go on thinking Nature can be defeated
It will leave our egos deflated
It will show us our assumption was wrong
That Nature was the ruler all along
You may read this poem and walk away
But just a minute, I've got something to say
Try to help, or you may die
The sun's favourite dish is human pie!

Nivethitha Ram (10)
Threemilestone School, Truro

Young Writers Information

We hope you have enjoyed reading this book - and that you will continue to enjoy it in the coming years.

If you like reading and writing poetry drop us a line, or give us a call, and we'll send you a free information pack.

Alternatively if you would like to order further copies of this book or any of our other titles, then please give us a call or log onto our website at
www.youngwriters.co.uk

**Young Writers Information
Remus House
Coltsfoot Drive
Peterborough
PE2 9JX**

(01733) 890066